The Last Long Pastorate

The Last Long Pastorate

A JOURNEY OF GRACE

F. Dean Lueking

WILLIAM B. EERDMANS PUBLISHING COMPANY
GRAND RAPIDS, MICHIGAN / CAMBRIDGE, U.K.

Wm. B. Eerdmans Publishing Co.

255 Jefferson Ave. S.E., Grand Rapids, Michigan 49503 /
P.O. Box 163, Cambridge CB3 9PU U.K.

Printed in the United States of America

07 06 05 04 03 02   7 6 5 4 3 2 1

ISBN 0-8028-3963-0

www.eerdmans.com

Contents

Introduction

My favorite story about long pastorates is about a crusty preacher who had tested a long-suffering congregation for years with his gruff manner in and out of the pulpit. One Sunday he startled the congregation by making an altogether unexpected announcement. After the benediction, he told the people to take their seats again to hear what he had to say. Striking his customary pose, hands on hips, brows knit in a frown, he fairly bellowed the news: "The Lord Jesus who brought me here thirty-four years ago is the same Lord Jesus who is calling me to another parish. I'm leaving!" He was hardly out of the chancel before the people arose in spontaneous exuberance to sing, "What a Friend We Have in Jesus."

On Pentecost Sunday several years ago, when I concluded my pastorate at Grace Lutheran Church, the one congregation I had served since my ordination forty-four years earlier, that grand old gospel hymn was not included, nor was the spirit of the day, I trust, akin to that of those folks who once sang it in happy relief. With deep thanks to God and to his extraordinary people of Grace Church, I have a different story to tell.

I tell my story for a reason. My sense is that long pastorates too often tend to be more tolerated, even lamented, than celebrated as a boon in the life of a church. The blight of staleness seems inevitable. People and pastor can settle into a satisfaction with the status quo that stifles creativity and narrows vision. The question arises whether twenty years in one place is blessed by a cumulative depth in ministry or cursed by a shallowness of one year's effort repeated twenty times over. Worst of all, long pastorates are too often the source of horror stories of pastors who stayed on far too long, who couldn't let go, and who made the lives of their successors miserable by meddling. Those things do happen. I have seen it, and the sight is sad beyond words.

But there are other stories to tell. When the chemistry of the Spirit between pastor and people is working, when the fit is right, when growth abounds in the ministry of the whole people of God in that place — then long pastorates are a unique gift to all who participate. Such stories need telling, and this is one of them. It is not the only one, by any means. But this is one that has its own unique cast and contours, joys and heartaches, failures and successes, and — I say it as a doxology — far more blessing than burden.

Is mine the *last* long pastorate? Are there not currently other pastorates equal to, and surpassing, my forty-four years at Grace Church? Of course there are. And will not others of similar duration come along? Of course they will — but not often. In fact, they are an increasing rarity. Any tenure longer than fifteen years in Protestant congregations these days approaches the long pastorate designation. Among Roman Catholics, pastoral assignments are on average shorter than Protestant ones, despite the critical shortage of priests that causes many to continue serving well after their planned retirement.

I speak of mine as the last long pastorate because of its uniqueness. My tenure of forty-four years at Grace was preceded by my predecessor's tenure of forty years; two pastors in one congregation for eighty-four years is anything but common! But more than the unusual longevity in years at Grace has been the quality of the grace at work through the particular times and circumstances, which are unrepeatable. In these chapters I wish to bear witness to the fascinating variety of opportunities for continuity and consistency in ministry in the latter half of the twentieth century, when change — often tumultuous, abrupt, and without breathing space — was the dominant theme in church and society. I want to share what I have learned through these decades. Though I have learned God's lessons best by staying put in one congregation, my hope is that the art and skills of ministry thus learned apply to pastors and congregations of any time and place.

The point of this book, then, is that what I have learned in what I call the last long pastorate is far more lasting than my own particular experience, and it is meant for the encouragement of all. This book is an appeal for a wider appreciation of continuity in parish ministry and a more ready welcoming of the gifts it offers to the whole church. It is not limited to the few colleagues who stay put without burning out or becoming dinosaurs; it can apply to pastors and people just getting started together or to those who are at some midpoint in their vocational journey. What endures, and why, and how? Also, what changes precisely because of the wisdom gained through longevity? This, I hope, is an insight of no small importance in this story.

This last long pastorate of mine has not ended. My ministry continues following the Grace years in ways and in places I would never have imagined (I touch on this briefly in the Epilogue). The post-Grace experience is testimony to the positive and mutually nurturing ties that flourish between my pastoral successor and me — with the congregation as the main beneficiary. There is something instructive here. Long-term experience, when blended with the freshness and energy of new pastoral gifts, can create — and is creating — needed documentation that retirement need not mean the amputation of well-defined, faithfully understood guidelines that glorify God and enrich everyone involved. In my view, there is a great need for this witness to reach far and wide throughout the land and well beyond.

The setting for this memoir is Grace Lutheran Church in the Chicago suburb of River Forest, Illinois. The occasion that prompts it is the centennial of that congregation, which they celebrate in 2002. I write with the hope of handing on a tradition of pastor and people, flawed though we are, yet seeking to do with excellence the ministry of the Word given us by a Lord who has given his best for us. These chapters describe that legacy — its origins, testings, joys, defeats, surprises, commonplaces, and enduring power from one generation to another. My story begins in the mid-1950s, when my ordination took place amid boom times for churches in America. It continues through decades that required a deep draw on the power of the gospel for sustenance through convulsive change, trivia and substance in theology and pastoral practice, growth through trials and errors, and, above all, savoring the matchless privilege of loving and being loved by God's people of Grace.

My predecessor in the Grace pastorate, the mentor from whom I learned so much, was Otto Geiseman. My successor, the gifted shepherd who now continues the Grace legacy in what I hope will be a long and grace-filled pastorate, is Bruce Modahl. To both I dedicate this pastoral memoir with gratitude and affection.

F. DEAN LUEKING
Epiphany, 2002

CHAPTER I

Ordination Day:
A Pastoral Ministry Begins

...and do you promise to adorn the gospel with a holy life?

The promise to adorn the gospel with a holy life is asked of all ordinands in the Lutheran Rite. That promise became mine to make on a sunlit day in August 1954 at Grace Lutheran Church in the Chicago suburb of River Forest, Illinois.

But that Sunday the adornment more on my mind than a holy life was the loose-fitting white clergy gown I wore and the white-buck shoes on my feet. I had been informed only the day before of the summer vestment tradition at Grace Church, which was white gown with clergy stole and white shoes — to be worn from Memorial Day through Labor Day. It made sense in that pre-air-conditioning era, when staying cool had to be more a matter of appearance than of air temperature. The gowns were well made by Mrs. Birnemann, an expert seamstress from the nearby Austin neighborhood of Chicago, who always seemed to speak out of the corner of her mouth after all those years of holding straight pins clamped between her lips. It was the white shoes, however, that made me self-conscious; I had not worn them since the age of three.

Now, two months past turning twenty-six, late on that Saturday afternoon in August, I had to hustle down to Tom McCann's on Lake Street in Oak Park to buy the last pair of white shoes they had in my size. They were not simply white: they were blinding white, their thick reddish soles only accentuating the whiteness and drawing greater attention to my feet. To add to my discomfort, the soloist for the ordination service, Elfrieda Miller of the Grace School faculty, sang "How Beautiful Are the Feet of Them That Preach Glad Tidings of Peace." Kneeling at the altar, I kept my eyes shut through most of my ordination vows, as if somehow to block out the embarrassment of my white bucks, which now seemed to be approaching the size of Greenland. I finally opened my eyes because the assistant pastor, Martin Marty, was nudging me with the ordination certificate he had been trying to put in my hands. Nobody, of course, noticed the white bucks but me. Nobody smiled at my discomfort. Nobody fainted. I didn't die. My ordination service was genuinely inspiring to me, as well as to my parents and family, who were seated in the first pew. After nine years of theological education, my pastoral ministry was underway. I was happy, excited, and relieved.

That August 15 Ordination Sunday had welcome touches of a Grace Church tradition about which I was to learn much more: the intention to do things well, with an understated fitness and elegance — if the latter word doesn't imply too much of an upper-middle-class snootiness that is often associated with life in River Forest. A reception in the Fellowship Hall followed the two morning services, giving parishioners an opportunity to welcome me, the new assistant pastor, and to say goodbye to the outgoing assistant pastor couple, Martin and Elsa Marty. After proper tributes to the Martys, Otto Geiseman, the Grace Church senior pastor and preacher of the day, spoke welcoming words to me. Then, on behalf of the congregation, he presented me with a striking silver cross, handmade for my ordination and designed by Marty with references to my interest in the world mission of the church: the cross was mounted on a flat circular sphere, hollowed inside, symbolizing the global reach of the gospel that I had grown to appreciate during a two-year vicarage in Japan prior to my seminary graduation.

As I shook the many hands and heard the many gracious words, my eye caught two ten-year-olds examining the cross, which was displayed handsomely on a black velvet cloth. I overheard one, eyebrows lifted in admiration, say, "Hey, neat cross, huh?" The other replied, "I think it's a bottle opener." The reception was elegant, and I liked the light touch of the boys' conversation as well. Later, at the parsonage dinner table, Pastor Geiseman and his wife, Marie, helped dispel most of whatever nervousness we Kansas City Luekings might have felt as their guests. My mother, as she told me later, did not feel fully comfortable until near the end of the meal, when Marie jumped up with a start and said, "Mercy! I forgot the rolls."

A late-afternoon moment of that day comes back to me whenever I pass along the 900 block of Franklin Street, where my parents and I parked for conversation after a brief tour of River Forest. Across the street from where we parked was the epitome of River Forest affluence, a home built by the Grunow family of the refrigerator fortune. Tony Accardo, also known as "Big Tuna" in the Chicago Mafia, was the current owner, a detail we did not know at the time. Nor did I know then, of course, that not many years later I would perform the wedding of the Accardo daughter, and would prepare her and her husband for membership in Grace Church. What I felt as we toured the streets of River Forest was more curiosity than awe regarding the opulence of some of the River Forest homes. What kinds of people lived in these magnificent homes? How could a newly ordained, rookie assistant pastor find access to their minds and souls?

Before long I would begin to get answers as I knocked on doors in this western Chicago suburb of 12,000. River Forest had a prominent Methodist church, a small but staid Episcopal church, a still smaller congregation of Plymouth Brethren, one large Roman Catholic Church on the southern edge of town (where the Northwestern tracks separate River Forest from Forest Park) and another Catholic church, St. Vincent's, soon to build an imposing new building and school on North Avenue (which forms the border between River Forest and Elmwood Park to the north). Western Chicago suburbia, at least in our region, did not have "towns," I soon learned; the designation is *village*, implying quaintness combined with sophistication and the taxes that go with it. To the east was Oak Park, four times the size of River Forest and famous for the legacy of its two most famous native sons, Frank Lloyd Wright and Ernest Hemingway. Soon I would be making mission calls in the oft-visited studio house where Wright had begun his architecture career at the turn of the century. The Chamber of Commerce brochure featuring Hemingway celebrated his local origins but did not include his slur on Oak Park, that it was a community of "broad lawns and narrow minds."

Percy Julian, the pioneering African-American scientist who endured cross-burnings on his Oak Park lawn, had not been born in Oak Park but lived there long enough to help the village begin to break out of racial prejudice in the post–World War II years and become an enlightened community of leadership in suburban integration of the races. To the west of River Forest lay Melrose Park, with its huge harness racing track and growing Italian population, and Maywood, with its diverse but not yet integrated black and white populations. I would learn much more about the attitudes, code words, fears, virtues, and foibles of the residents of all these communities. Many of the 1,300 baptized members of Grace Lutheran came from addresses in all of them, others lived in Chicago, and a scattering in several dozen more distant suburbs.

That late afternoon of August 15, 1954, however, was not a time for urban sociology conversation. It was a time for my parents and me to enjoy the events of this day that would be long remembered — the Geiseman sermon, the power of congregational singing, the prayers for my ministry, the beauty of the sanctuary with its majestic altar and the stained-glass windows around the nave, the hospitality we received in the Fellowship Hall and parsonage, and the white summer gown and white bucks. These recollections of that day forty-eight years ago have their share of trivia; but I include them because of my conviction that the Infinite does dwell among things finite. I don't recall all the words spoken to me that day, and the text and sermon have also slipped my memory. What stays with me is the feel of that day of pastoral beginnings. If the word "blessing" is not too overused, let it evoke the biblical picture of a cup running over with the sheer abundance of divine lovingkindness and steadfast mercy — Christ-centered and inseparable from God's people.

The three of us, parents and newly ordained son, sitting together in grateful conversation in the church Plymouth I had just inherited, offer a parable on the blessing of the day, on all that preceded it, and on all that would follow. Sleep came quickly to me after such a full day, but later that night, during a heavy thunderstorm, a bolt of lightning struck the power line just outside my tiny room on the third floor of the Oak Park YMCA. The sharp crack of lightning and the shower of sparks that shot up outside my window brought me bolt upright in bed and gave me an instant to wonder if this impromptu sound-and-light show was God's metaphor for the ministry I was beginning. In ways I was too sleepy to think about at the moment, it was.

I had arrived in Chicago two weeks prior to my ordination in order to get settled in. Recently graduated from Concordia Seminary in St. Louis, I had taken the train from my home in Kansas City, and had gotten off at the Dearborn Street station with bag and baggage in hand. I was excited when I recognized Otto Geiseman, the longtime and much-respected pastor of the Grace congregation, whom I had seen and heard once before — when he had come to Concordia Seminary to lecture on preaching. His greeting was genuine. I can see him clearly in my mind's eye: neatly dressed in a gray suit, clergy collar, and a Panama straw hat — a heartening sight as I dealt with jitters as well as hopes for what lay ahead. He shook my hand firmly and greeted me warmly. In response to his question about where the rest of my gear might be, I mumbled something about bachelors traveling light. But I quickly added that my books were coming separately, hoping to compensate for the two smallish suitcases I was carrying. He took my arm reassuringly, and to this day I recall how much the power of touch means for positive beginnings.

Off we went to the dining room of the Gremere Hotel, handsome with its walls of deep green, windows in white trim, the ample breakfast menu that was not only printed but in a leatherbound covering, and a saucer under the bone china coffee cup. Don Eckdahl was in charge of this breakfast meeting, the first Grace parishioner I had met. He welcomed me with just the right touch of warmth and understated formality. During breakfast Pastor Geiseman steered the conversation toward the things that mattered in my life rather than immediately listing what I was expected to do. His manner was friendly, wonderfully free of airs, and yet marked by an instinctive dignity that laid the groundwork for our solid relationship, which only deepened and expanded until his death eight years later.

When we reached Grace's parking lot, adjacent to the south lawn of the church with space for a dozen cars, we pulled in just as Chris Garbers was getting out of his car. He was a man in his seventies and, though I did not know it at the time, one of the key people who had helped to make the church what it had become by the mid-1950s, a congregation that reflected much of what gospel-centered community is about — faith active in love. He had been there to welcome young Otto Geiseman to the Grace pastorate in 1922; he had been a supporter of the controversial move from worship in German to English in the mid-1920s; and he had provided leadership for the planning of the new Grace Church and School in River Forest in the late '20s. He was among those who had celebrated the dedication of the new facilities in 1931 and the burning of the mortgage in 1945 after the hard, heroic years of stewardship through the Great Depression. He stood there, modest in manner but with a twinkle in his eye, as Pastor Geiseman introduced him as "Mr. Grace Church." His current role, after so many years of service and leadership in the congregation, was that of mission outreach leader. Before long he and I would be spending much time together, garnering the names and addresses of newcomers in the neighborhood and preparing messages of invitation to Grace Church.

This modest, quietly effective, steadily faithful man was the second parishioner I met within hours of arriving in Chicago on July 31, 1954, and I could not have been more fortunate in meeting him. What I had no way of knowing as we chatted briefly in the church parking lot was that his beloved 19-year-old grandson, preparing to be a teacher in Lutheran schools, was within a few weeks of death from cancer. Much lay beneath the surface pleasantries. Otto Geiseman knew about it but waited for a later, better time to inform me of such matters and what it meant to serve people deep in the shadow of death's dark valley.

Pastor Geiseman took me into the pastor's study and invited me to sit in the chair alongside his handsome oak desk. Leaning back in his chair after a brief pause to light a cigar (this was 1954), he looked squarely in my eyes and said, "Dean, there's one thing I'd like to get straight between us right off the bat." I thought I could finish the sentence with things that seminarians fresh out of the box need to hear: don't rock the boat, have the sense to listen more than talk, and get a feel for the congregation before trying to revise it from top to bottom. Nothing of the sort. What he said was: "We're not doing everything around here as best the Lord would have it done. So, whatever you see that we've missed, whatever creative ideas you can bring that we haven't thought of, whatever encouragement and critique you can come up with that will exalt Christ and build us up — don't wait around. Pitch in now because we need you and want you. And one more thing: that's why we're paying you enormous amounts of money" ($125 a month, plus car and housing).

He meant every word of this opening statement that thrilled me to my toes, and he confirmed it in practice. An example: mission calls to newcomers and others in the area were made mainly by the pastors. A key biblical theme for me in defining the task of the pastor was "to equip the saints for the work of ministry," in St. Paul's words from Ephesians 4:12. Within the first few months after my ordination, I offered a plan to do that. No one was stronger than Geiseman in recommending it to the congregation, nor clearer in emphasizing that the idea was mine. His gift for bringing out the best in everyone, of recognizing and respecting distinctive gifts, of working together for the good that is greater than any one of us, of growing in mutual love and sharing it beyond the congregation, of *enjoying* the ministry and helping colleagues do the same — those were gifts that blessed me from Day One.

My beginning at Grace, like beginnings in all things that matter, was of critical importance. It set the tone for a Geiseman-Lueking relationship that over the eight years of serving together grew in mutual respect, common theological ground, and even honest sharing of differences from time to time. But I do not recall five minutes of bitterness or rancor during our shared ministry. Despite our age difference of thirty-five years, I found that gap more of an asset than a barrier because of the accumulated wisdom he had gained from a pastoral vocation that had begun in downstate Illinois and had flowered during his forty-year pastorate at Grace.

Geiseman had come to a divisive Grace Church in 1922: the congregation had done in the three previous pastors since its founding in 1902 as a daughter congregation of St. John's Lutheran Church in Forest Park. Soon after his arrival, a defining moment for Geiseman as pastor occurred at his first Christmas Eve service. An anonymous, mean-spirited letter appeared on his desk when he arrived that evening, and as he later recounted, he made the mistake of opening it before the service. On second thought, he added, perhaps it was better that he did read it before the service. It gave him the opportunity to do something he had never done before or after. Following the benediction, he asked the congregation to be seated. He told them that he would read them the letter accusing him of God knows what, and that if even one member would rise to support its contents, he would resign on the spot. He read the letter. No one stood up or raised even a head, an arm, or a hand. Without further ado, he wished the startled people of Grace Church a merry Christmas with their children and families, and went home to do the same with his.

No moment like that had ever happened in the two decades of this church's life that had been beset by legalistic wrangling, which had made the name Grace a misnomer for this unhappy company of German Lutherans trying to keep their language, their Missouri Synod identity, and their parish school afloat through the stoutly anti-German years of World War I in America. Geiseman's defining moment said something about a pastoral leadership that was secure enough in the gospel to confront people with the reality of what happens when hearers of the Word are not doers.

What gave Geiseman his strength as a servant leader was the gospel itself. He put into practice what we now call a "mission statement" of just eight words: "Our aim, save souls; our means, the gospel." His centering of pastoral and congregational ministry in the freeing power of the gospel rather than the stifling effect of legalism imbued him with something I soon learned to admire and emulate: creative fidelity.

8

Geiseman taught me creativity. He saw the need for healing congregational rifts by addressing them openly and honestly, clarifying that it is the gospel that is always at stake. He helped the parishioners make the creative move from German to English so that the congregation could begin to add names such as Basilio Cimaglio, who chaired the finance committee for the new Grace Church, as well as many more who were not of German heritage. In 1927 he motivated the congregation to act on the creative vision of a much finer and vastly expanded sanctuary and school in River Forest, and to see the challenge through by building it and paying for it. He kept the creative spirit alive in his own spiritual and academic growth, earning his doctorate at Chicago Lutheran Seminary through part-time study right through the years of maximum demand on his time and energies as a pastor, husband, and father of six children. He initiated a program of two-year assistant pastors in the late 1940s, a program utterly unique in the Missouri Synod at the time. He made his case successfully to reluctant synodical and seminary officials, thus opening the door to many of us who were to get our pastoral bearings under his mentoring — along with gaining the long-term benefit of graduate study for vocational enrichment.

Pastor Geiseman also taught me theological faithfulness. His creative ministry was anchored in fidelity to the gospel as witnessed by Scripture, given by God through the mystery of the Holy Spirit's inspiration, to build up believers for mission in the daily life of the world. Through decades when much of American Protestantism was rocked by the liberal-conservative debate over the authority of Scripture, Geiseman was not drawn into that battle: he believed that scriptural authority was centered in the gospel, not for hair-splitting but for ministry to real people facing life's realities. That foundation did not shift from generation to generation or age to age. By hearing him preach three Sundays out of four each month, sitting in on his adult instruction classes, listening to his reflections on pastoral counseling, and watching him combine faithfulness to the Word with care for people in parish meetings, I learned things not taught in seminaries and relished the experience of working with him.

His creative fidelity, not surprisingly, also brought him under fire.

There were preachers who went after him because they bristled at his blunt opposition to legalistic practices that stifled the gospel, such as those forbidding prayer with other Lutherans, indeed any other Christians except those of the Lutheran Church–Missouri Synod. At one pastoral conference held at nearby Trinity Lutheran Church in Oak Park, I saw him lose patience with argumentative wrangling. He rose and said simply, "There's nothing wrong with you, brethren, that reading a new book and getting your pants pressed wouldn't help." He could also defuse a tense moment with humor, as my predecessor in the assistant chair at Grace Church learned when a dozen or so pastors engaged in an attack on Geiseman in what was called a Winkel Conference (*Winkel* is German for "corner," thus pastors from around the corner). While fending off thunderbolts from left and right around the table, Geiseman noticed that Martin Marty was lighting up a cigar to reduce tension in the room. Geiseman wrote a note on a slip of paper and had it passed from man to man to Marty at the opposite end of the table. The consensus around the table was that the old dog was surely coaching the young pup in some new heresy or slick maneuver. Marty opened the note and read: "You lit the wrong end."

Geiseman taught me not only creative fidelity in the pastoral calling in the church but also critical appreciation for the pastor's place in the community. He encouraged me to join the local ministerial association for broader ecumenical contacts and the Oak Park Optimist Club, which he had joined years before. That enabled me to get to know area businesspeople, and it put me in touch with community life through their eyes as I listened to their noonday lunch conversations around the table. I had my first experience in serving on a board of directors of a social work agency as well as membership on a Missouri Synod committee on church history publications through his example and encouragement. Though the Missouri Synod in which he was a lifelong pastor never was comfortable with him at its top levels, he served with critical loyalty on the board of directors of that church body — and taught me by his example. He wrote a monthly column in another critically loyal magazine that was an unofficial publication of the Missouri Synod, *The American Lutheran.* It was helpful for me during my start-up period to read back issues and catch the flavor of his steady commentary on the virtues and foibles of church and society, always seen through the lens of parish ministry. That Geiseman talent opened another window and provided another directive: parish pastors should write, and do so without apology for being "only a parish pastor."

One unexpected, early experience of the world invading the church came in a surprise encounter with a man who had broken into the Grace Church office one summer evening not long after my August ordination. We bumped into each other at the church door, which I had locked earlier when I left for mission calls in the neighborhood. I asked him what he was doing inside, and he told me that he was looking for our janitor, Felix. But when I saw that the glass panel was broken in the upper half of the church office door, and also noticed that there was blood on his knuckles, even I got the message that something was amiss. I moved to call the police on the office phone. He moved to exit, muttering something about getting his "car out of the no parking zone on the street." I put down the phone, and we walked out of the building — wordless. But my heart was pounding as I wondered what I was getting myself into. At our church corner he bolted across Division Street for the Dominican Priory grounds. On blind instinct, I ran after him and brought him down from behind with a flying tackle of sorts. We scuffled on the curbside grass, and I yelled for help to passing motorists; they obviously wanted no part of this odd wrestling match. I finally lugged my quarry into the nearby Mobil station, where the astonished attendant called the police. After taking him off to the River Forest lockup, the detective took me back to the scene of the scuffle, where he picked up a sizable switchblade that had fallen from the malefactor's pocket. I remember the look on his face and his scolding tone as he held up the switchblade and said: "You don't know how lucky you are, Rev'ner, because you sure don't look like the fighting type."

After answering questions, dusting myself off, and removing my grass-stained clerical collar, I called at the Geiseman parsonage door to report on the evening's activities. The pastor and his wife were entertaining guests, but as I stepped out of the shadows of the front steps,

Geiseman did a double take and ushered me to the kitchen. When I showed him a fair-sized bite on my right wrist, a trophy of my evening in darkest River Forest, he went straightway to the kitchen cabinet and poured out a full cup of Jim Beam. He informed me that this was the standard medicine I was to take against the germs of the human bite. I swallowed it, turning redder by the gulp, and followed his next instruction, which was to go to the emergency room of West Suburban Hospital. When I checked in for a tetanus shot, sans clerical collar, the resident (who, I noticed, wore white bucks) took one whiff of my breath well doused in bourbon, and in a world-weary tone asked for my name and occupation. In deliberately slowed, if not slurred words, I told him that I was "the new assis-tant pas-tor at Gr-ace Luth-er-an Chur-ch." He looked up, smelled my breath again, looked down at the bite wound again, and, incredulous at the thought, gave me the tetanus shot and sent me home.

Some days later I visited the Cook County Jail, my first of many visits, and was admitted to the cell of the man whose switchblade, mercifully, had stuck in the ground where we had wrestled rather than in me. He was my age, married, with a family back in Columbus, Ohio, where he was also wanted for breaking and entering. During our conversation, he asked me to do something about the charges pending against him in Ohio, which I could not do. But shifting the conversation to the charges before another Judge, I offered him the assurance that those charges indeed have been settled, once and for all, at the high cost of a cross. He accepted the New Testament I had brought and the prayer I offered for him, his family, and his future. We shook hands, and I left the jail. He stayed.

That moment has stuck with me: here were two men, the same age, brothers in the human family, both of us known and named by God through baptism, and yet worlds apart in background and present circumstances of life. Walking out of the Cook County Jail, as I heard the steel doors clang shut — one after the other as I passed the cells with vacant eyes staring out at me — I had reason to think of how much I had to learn about the world in which I was to join the church in ministry. I had grown up in a city, had lived during my Japan vicarage close to the docks and houseboats for the homeless in Yokohama, and had spent a summer helping to build a dormitory in Mainz, Germany, for refugee youth from Communist East Germany. I had already circled the world, but I had so much to learn about the world that exists between the ears and in the hearts of every human being, including the one who tried to get into Grace Church the hard way one August evening.

My ordination came in the heart of the Eisenhower years, dubbed the "era of good feeling" in America. For churches, particularly of the Protestant mainline (Methodist, Presbyterian, Congregational, Baptist), it was a time of rapid growth, heady expectations, and denominational prowess. Amid this often triumphalist atmosphere, there was hardly a hint of the chaotic upheavals soon to erupt in the coming two decades. I certainly had no clue about what would affect my ministry full force in the 1960s and 1970s. These mid-1950s were salad days for the church. On the Monday afternoon and evening after my ordination day, I plunged in with rookie zeal, making sixteen mission calls on families from our mission list, and thinking nothing of the number of calls or the assumptions behind this method of outreach. Congregational growth was a given at this time, but I sensed that it did not happen with preachers staying in the church office all day. People tended to follow their own denominations since they were part of the boom days of the church in suburbia. My job was to find them. Billy Graham was fast becoming the best-known preacher in America; vast numbers of Americans were filling stadiums and auditoriums to make decisions for Christ. This approach was foreign to Lutherans: we were not good at mass evangelism. Our way was doorbell to doorbell; we were more inclined to invite to church rather than to invite to Christ within the first few minutes of meeting a stranger.

Beneath the differences in approach and theology in this era of good feeling, however, was a deeper common denominator of unofficial theology and unacknowledged assumptions. A few months after my ordination, Will Herberg published *Catholic, Protestant, Jew,* his widely read book that offered a framework for how most Americans saw the three major religious groups, buttressed by the pervasive idea that a single way of American life and ethos was evident in all three. The crusade against atheistic Communism provided another unifying influence nationally, attracting moderates as well as right-wing conservatives among Protestants and Catholics alike to form a common front against an ideological enemy. The old Federal Council of Churches had given way to the new and more inclusive National Council of Churches in 1951.

Closer to home, the Lutheran Council of Greater Chicago provided a network of cooperation among various Lutheran congregations for mission and social ministry. I recall attending gala dinner meetings that would bring a thousand Lutherans together in one place. I also began to attend the Oak Park–River Forest Ministerial Alliance's monthly meetings, which gave me an opportunity to meet other Protestant clergy of the area. Through its executive director, Rupert O'Brien, who also doubled as the director of the local YMCA, I had found my first place of residence after my arrival in River Forest: a room at the Y, where the cafeteria spared me my bachelor cooking and the swimming pool provided a space for frequent exercise.

I was only vaguely aware of the overarching religious milieu — locally and nationally — as I got my pastoral bearings. But I soon gained a sense that, to be somebody in River Forest or Oak Park in 1954, it certainly helped to be a member of a Congregational, Methodist, or Presbyterian church. Early on, I also learned that Grace Lutheran Church was not in that charmed circle, but that nobody at Grace seemed to notice or mind. We were still perceived as the mainly German-background folks who had a splendid Gothic church building, to be sure, and a parochial school of high reputation, but were still lumped together with Concordia Teachers College as outsiders to the real in-group who made things happen in our village. We were tightly linked with Concordia and had been since 1913, when the college moved to its campus on the one square block that church and college shared. Concordia paid the salaries of half the Grace School faculty in exchange for the latter institution's functioning as a laboratory school where many of the college students took their practice teaching. I vividly recall my bemused puzzlement over the comment of a parishioner who left Grace and "graduated" to the nearby Presbyterian church — that his reason for doing so was "the Concordia element."

As I saw my life's assignment to Grace Church on Ordination Sunday, I had the feeling of being truly favored among my 120 seminary classmates. The congregation appeared healthy to me by every definition. My mentor, Otto Geiseman, was in his prime years as pastor, thirty-two of them since coming to Grace. Victor Waldschmidt was in his seventh of twenty-three years of service as the principal of Grace School, where 360 children were enrolled, half of them from non-Lutheran families. Paul Bouman had come to the church the year before me, beginning three decades of a stellar ministry that combined full-time service as a Grace School teacher with his full-time calling as organist and director of adult and children's choirs. The janitorial couple, Felix and Martha Gutgesell, who had come to Grace as German immigrants in the 1930s, took care of the building as if it were their own.

But more important than their longevity of service was my impression that these people really *liked* being together without having to work at it, each doing what he or she did with a sort of matter-of-factness that did not require constant pulse-taking or even frequent meetings. If there were rifts and disgruntlement in the staff and congregation, which no doubt there were, they were well buried. The joy of Ordination Sunday was no fluke. I would have to meet tests, to be sure, but there was solid ground beneath me that happy August 15 as I began what I thought would be my two-year stint in the procession of Pastor Geiseman's assistants.

As it turned out, I was off by forty-two years.

CHAPTER 2

Family Foundations and Call

"Why am I a pastor? Because I have to . . ."

I do not come from a family line of preachers, at least not any who prefaced their names with Pastor, Reverend, Father, Bishop — or any other titles that indicate ministry as a profession. But my maternal grandfather was a lay minister of the first order, and his influence on me was subtle but effective as I was growing up.

My mother's side of the family were Missourians from the region where the Ozark hill country flattens out toward the southeast. My mother was born down there, in the town of Eldorado Springs, the middle child of seven in a devout family of the Reorganized Church of Jesus Christ of Latter Day Saints. Her name, Tyra Lloyd, reflected her Welsh ancestry; she was happy with Lloyd as her family name, but she lived with Tyra only because she disliked her middle name, Lucinda, even more. Her father, Evan Walter Lloyd, moved the family to Kansas City, Missouri, at the turn of the century to work for Standard Oil, making the rounds of his customers via horse and wagon. And he devoted much of his spare time to his real passion, his work as a lay minister in the RLDS.

When I was no more than eight years old, he would occasionally take me with him to conduct funerals for the nameless, homeless derelicts whose bodies had been delivered from the morgue to the Lapetina Funeral Home in Kansas City's rundown North End. He never owned nor drove a car, traveling instead by streetcar to deliver a full-length sermon to an audience that was often no more than himself and the rotund Mr. Lapetina — sometimes with me as the third one present, sitting there spooked and fascinated by the caskets and corpses in clear view. The signal for my grandfather to get to the Amen at the end of his funeral homily was when my legs, too short to reach the floor from the folding chair, would start swinging to keep the circulation going. I doubt that he ever received more than a dollar from Mr. Lapetina for ministerial services rendered, which were no less fervent — if not as professional — than those the ordained clergy might offer. "Daddy Lloyd," as everyone called grandfather, went whenever and wherever he was called to speak the Word to the known and unknown, never charging a fee. I was not fully aware of all that, but a lasting impression of ministry was beginning to form in me from someone who had never seen a seminary classroom nor read any book beyond the Bible or the Book of Mormon.

Another memory of "Daddy Lloyd's" early influence on me is vivid. When I was about ten, scarlet fever hit me hard — the second time around. The quarantine signs were no sooner up on our front door, a customary precaution in those pre-wonder-drug days of the early 1930s, than E. W. Lloyd was at my bedside. What I remember about the effects of my seriously high fever was hearing his voice as though from the end of a tunnel and squinting to see his face as though I were looking through a line of concentric circles. I was worried as he knelt beside me, wondering if I was as sick as his ministrations seemed to indicate. I recall a combination of curiosity and embarrassment as he anointed my head with oil and offered intercessory prayer. This was my early introduction to the biblical prescription in James 4:14-16 for the ministry of healing; and the ministry seemed to be efficacious: the fever gradually receded, leaving me alive and with no damage.

Another visitor that day was the formidable Dr. Aull, our family physician whose dour bedside manner was enough to scare me into recovery. He knew what he was doing as a general practitioner, having earned the confidence of my parents by being available for house calls at all hours. Here was another formative childhood experience that would later shape my belief and practice of the ministry of healing: intercessory prayer and stethoscope fit together; the oil of anointing and the capsules of medicine are partners in the larger realm of how God restores health. Not either/or, but both/and. Although there were no ordained pastors in my immediate family line, there were ministers even if they did not see themselves as such. My grandfather did pastoral work without a license or union card, and he gladly embraced his ministry. Dr. Aull, the capable grump with the black doctor's bag, would have growled at the very idea of being thought of as a minister of the healing Christ.

My father's side of the family was from Nebraska. He was one of twelve, the middle son among six sisters and five brothers, born of German Lutheran parents who homesteaded in the early 1880s near Oxford, in south-central Nebraska. He was baptized Friedrich Karl Lueking, which was shortened to Fred when he began the only schooling that was available there, a one-room schoolhouse near the Lueking homestead. His father, Henry Ernest, had come from a Wesphalian village east of Hanover, which he left in his late teens rather than be drafted into the German army and become cannon fodder for wars he thought were useless. As a Nebraska farmer, he shipped Herefords each year to the Kansas City stockyards, taking one son along with him as each came of age. My father's turn came in 1912. Following the sale of cattle, Father Lueking took his son on a streetcar ride, thinking the boy with the bright red hair would be properly awed by the truly up-to-date nature of sights in Kansas City. Whatever else young Fred saw, one sight in particular caught and held his eye: a tall, slender brunette, her hair gathered in a large red bow, was seated several seats ahead of him on the streetcar.

As my father later told the story, he was much too shy to do anything other than admire the young woman's striking good looks — and dream about her during the year that passed on the Lueking farm. He returned to Kansas City with his father in 1913, again sold the cattle, got on the same streetcar as they had the year before, hoping against hope that he might see the face he had not forgotten. To his astonishment, he did. Just as was true the year before, she was on her way to an after-school job in a bread bakery, where her older sister was in charge of employment. This time the red-haired farm boy followed the city girl with the red bow in her hair into the bakery, asked for a job, and got it. Then he set about toward his real goal, which was not necessarily working in a bakery but meeting Tyra Lucinda Lloyd. As it turned out, he succeeded at both. On the first count, he began a lifelong bread sales career with the General Baking Company in Kansas City.

In order to improve his chances of courting Tyra in an era of mounting anti-German sentiment, Fred did not tell Tyra that his name was Friedrich Karl, or even Fred, but Clarence — the most American of names that came to his mind. But before they were engaged and he went off to serve in the Marine Corps during World War I, he did own up to his baptismal name. Their sixty-two-year marriage was a miracle of contrasts. Mother was a city girl, of Welsh ancestry, active in her RLDS congregation, and a well-educated public school teacher in Kansas City, who had a lifelong love of reading, gave book reviews around the city, and was gifted in writing letters that were literary gems. The lethal flu epidemic of 1918 had cost her all but 20 percent of her hearing, a handicap she turned into an asset by wearing a hearing aid, learning lip reading, and becoming one of the first teachers of deaf children and adults in Kansas City.

Father was a Nebraska farm boy, formally educated up to high school, of sturdy German Lutheran church life, a transplant to the city where he excelled as a bread salesman. Sometimes he bumped into Harry S. Truman when the latter ran a haberdashery shop on Twelfth Street in downtown Kansas City. He could fix most anything, and he put his early training in farm machinery maintenance to good use in keeping our household humming.

Among the many things my mother gave me, her love of literature and a care for words stand out. She hovered over me at homework time, making sure that my spelling, syntax, and flow of language met her high standards. Her courage in the face of her hearing impediment complemented her empathy for those marginalized by any disabling impairment, especially the deaf, whose odd-sounding speaking voices and sign-language communication have too often been the butt of cruel mimicry. She also humored me and my neighborhood pals by allowing us to watch, awestruck, as she answered the telephone by placing the old bell-shaped phone receiver not to her ear but to the hearing aid speaker clipped beneath her blouse.

Prominent among the character genes my father passed down to me was his capacity for perseverance: he would stick with what he was doing until it was done, often despite my mother's calls from the kitchen that supper was ready. He would station me beside him to hold the extension-cord light as he worked under the hood of our 1936 Plymouth, which had to make it through 1945 during the World War II years of car and fuel shortage. And he was not amused one time when, in the middle of the street where the fading blue Plymouth had died, I audibly admired a shiny new Pontiac that whizzed around us and up the steep hill we were about to roll back down. I was not much of a mechanic, but he made me stick with it until I learned some things about motor and house repair.

My father persevered with the customers on his bread delivery route. Sometimes, when I was a teenager, he would take me along on his predawn rounds that included people as varied as upscale hotel restaurant managers, Greek cooks in six-stool sandwich shops, grocerymen whose names and bread orders he knew well, and Negro (never "nigger") proprietors of Kansas City's famed jazz clubs along East Twelfth Street. He persevered in his suffering of bruised shins when he functioned as the catcher of my wild southpaw pitches. I would wait for him, ball glove in hand, to pull in the driveway after my school was out and his fourteen-hour workday was over.

One event that pushed my father's perseverance over the edge, however, was when his pastor at Immanuel Lutheran Church refused him Holy Communion at the altar rail and lectured him then and there about his joining the Teamsters Union in 1933. Pastor Theodore Schwartz typified a Germanic idolization of authority when he damned labor unions as a defiance of management authority — management that was causing

Fred Lueking to work fourteen to sixteen hours a day, six days a week. For several years thereafter, my father persevered at Sunday morning golf — until a pastoral change meant a new day at Immanuel Church.

Different though my parents were, each gave me distinctive gifts. Together they gave me and my sister, Donnis, an early example of ecumenicity. How that worked out was another moment of serendipity. My sister and I had gone to the Lutheran church before the Teamsters uproar; but while father was in his Sunday golfing leave of absence from heavy-handed pastoral mistreatment, our mother took us to the RLDS church for worship and Sunday school. That tradition, however, had no Christmas Eve services. Like all Lutheran churches, Immanuel did, and we went as a family. My dad's offhand remark to the effect that it would be wonderful if seven-year-old Dean could be in the Christmas Eve program was enough to move Mom to agree that that would be nice. And thus by lateral pass I was transferred from Mrs. Worden's Sunday school class at the RLDS Fourth Church to Mrs. Engelbart's class at Immanuel Lutheran. Donnis remained in the RLDS congregation.

With that act — and without my knowing it — I became a Lutheran. Making the switch was helped in that T. A. Weinhold had just come to Immanuel as the new pastor: he not only reclaimed my father into the fold but also formed a lifelong, respectful spiritual tie with my mother. Though I had been baptized at Immanuel, I remember nothing about that congregation until I began attending Sunday school there after the Christmas Eve decision, and later my confirmation instruction under Pastor Weinhold's exemplary pastoral leadership. Sometimes we attended Sunday worship together as a family. But more often it was Dad and I trudging up the steep hill off Forty-second and Paseo to Immanuel Church, its handsome sandstone exterior crowned by a neon cross of garish green, while Mom and Donnis went off to Central Congregation of the RLDS. Actually, our family church life seemed to benefit from this arrangement rather than disintegrate into going nowhere mutually.

I credit my parents with making the Lueking household good soil for the seeds of faith and love to take hold. My earliest memory of hearing Bible stories was from Mother Tyra, who would tell me of Jesus, especially of his cross and resurrection, while she ironed in the kitchen of our home on Troostwood Road. My first experiences of prayer go back to when I was four, to Sunday morning, the one morning of the week that Father Fred could sleep in. I would zoom into my parents' bedroom like a guided missile, dive into bed between them, and hear the Sunday morning funnies from the *Kansas City Star.* Feeling the warmth of their bodies beside me, I would recite after my father, *Abba, lieber Vater, macht mich fromm, dass ich bei dir in Himmel komm,* a child's prayer asking the dear Father above to make me worthy of coming to him in heaven. Mother would follow by leading me, line by line, in prayers that taught me to love the Jesus about whose cross I heard from her at the ironing board. She noticed a table prayer from the child's magazine, *Wee Wisdom,* that we prayed as a family at mealtime. Our family still prays the prayer today, seventy years later, and we've added it to the treasury of prayers our grandchildren have learned.

Another chance event contributed to a foundation for my pastoral vocation. In 1937 the director of the boys choir at Grace and Holy Trinity Episcopal Cathedral was allowed to audition among the treble voices at my school, Frances Willard Public School. An announcement of this interesting cooperation between church and public school was sent to the homes of all the boys in my class. I was not interested, but my mother was. And because of her interest, I was obliged to show up at the after-school audition conducted by Mabel Glenn, whose crisp, professional manner put me on my best behavior. I was accepted, to my initial chagrin — because it meant Saturday morning rehearsals for two hours at the downtown Cathedral as well as singing each Sunday at the eleven o'clock choral Eucharist. I had to get used to the Saturday rehearsals and the Sunday morning streetcar rides to the cathedral, always after our own early service and Sunday school at Immanuel. It added up to a long weekend, but I learned superb choral music and heard Bishop Robert Nelson Spencer preach regularly. What nearly did me in was the red cassock, white surplices, and large, red-collar bows that were the required vestments of the boys choir. For the years until my voice changed, I lived in fear of my school and ball team friends catching sight of me processing down the cathedral aisle in those required vestments. No such thing happened, of course, and I carried with me from that early time a permanent love and appreciation for the music of faith that has stood the test of the centuries.

My call to the pastoral ministry was not a planned event, simply one more in that great chain of mysteries whereby the Holy Spirit makes the most routine habit an occasion on which the course of a lifetime turns. I spent the summers during my high school years working on the Robert Timm farm in northern Illinois. Matilda Timm was my father's younger sister, and her husband, Bob, was patient with me as a city kid who had quickly fallen in love with farm life in that soil-rich region several hours west of Chicago. The Timms had a son, Wallace, for whom I functioned as a summertime stand-in older brother and boyhood chum. The Timm family never missed Sunday morning worship at nearby Immanuel Lutheran Church in Lindenwood, where Edwin Schulenberg, another of my uncles, was the pastor. Schulenberg played a large role in my Illinois summers on the farm, as a pastor but more particularly as a pitcher on the seminary baseball team in earlier years; he had a fastball lively enough to catch the attention of Major League scouts. However, he turned that prospect down and became a pastor who made many a Sunday afternoon memorable for me. He would teach me how to throw a good curve ball as we played catch, and then, sitting under a tree in the backyard of the parsonage, tell me stories about the pastoral life. He never told me that I ought to choose the pastoral vocation. But somehow in those frequent conversations he was laying the groundwork for my call, groundwork that had been established earlier by parental example, a grandfather's lay ministry, Sunday school teachers, T. A. Weinhold in my home congregation, the Episcopal Cathedral Boys Choir experience, and even the National Radio Pulpit broadcast of Ralph Sockman's sermons — regular fare in the Lueking kitchen after church every Sunday as my mother prepared the Sabbath staple menu of roast beef and brown gravy.

The fourth Sunday in August 1945 dawned bright and clear. The nation at large was digesting a complex mix of events: the simultaneous celebration of the end of World War II and the horrific atomic bombing of Hiroshima and Nagasaki, unquestioned by many as decisive in ending it. In my small corner of the universe, it was an unusual Sunday, somewhat outside the lockstep routine on the Timm farm of the morning milking and feeding chores that had to be done in time to get to church. The day before, we had cut acres of alfalfa and windrowed it in long, neat lines across the fields, where it dried before we were to load it on the wagon and store it in the barn. For me it was exciting and fun: the sweet smell of new-mown hay being piled up behind me in stacks twice my height by Uncle Robert, who was behind me on the hayrack with pitchfork in hand to balance the mounting load. The weather was perfect. The trusty pair of sorrels were faultless in pulling the hayrack, not getting feisty even when they felt my inexperienced hand on the lines. As a city boy just turned seventeen, I relished the satisfaction of being part of the farm's work team on a busy day. Those memories all come back to me as the ones I thought I would most retain from that day. But they were not.

My uncle, Pastor Schulenberg, had arranged for a mission festival service for the evening of that last Sunday in August. These services were fairly common, especially in rural and small-town Lutheran parishes: they usually featured a guest preacher, and sometimes members of neighboring congregations would come together to hear about the preaching of the Word in places near and far. The preacher that evening was to be a young chaplain from Camp Grant, a half hour away on the outskirts of Rockford. Robert and Matilda Timm, my farm "parents," announced that we all would attend and should have ourselves scrubbed and changed in time for the ringing of the church bell promptly at 7:30 p.m. My recollections are that I was not overly thrilled about this compulsory arrangement. I was tired out from a full day's work and would have been happy to have stayed home, where I could ride Mike, the black-and-white pinto pony, or cool off in the horse tank, which subbed as a mini–swimming pool. But it was not a matter of choice. So at 7:10, I got into the car with Wallace, bound for church and not at all expecting that my life would be changed in the next two hours.

Chaplain Martin Werfelmann preached on the Parable of the Sower and the Seed, focusing on the need for sowers in a world that cried out for the seed of the gospel. I listened as intently as my energies allowed after a long day of work in the field. The sermon prepared me for the concluding hymn, No. 496 in the old Lutheran Hymnal, "Hark the Voice of Jesus Calling." The first stanza ends with a question about who will answer the Master's call to labor in fields ripe for harvest, who will say, "Here am I, send me, send me?" In the fourth stanza the question is turned around to become a declaration of response to the question: "Here am I, send me, send me!" While I was singing that declaration, it took hold. Those seven words framed a moment when my mind and spirit, until then quite undecided about whether to study law or agricultural engineering or whatever, were touched by God's Spirit — who had pastoral ministry in mind for me. No chills ran up and down my spine, nor did the "Send me" phrase in the hymn hit me like a lightning bolt. I quietly closed the hymnal, received the benediction, went back to the farm, and slept well. When I arose the next morning, I wrote a postcard home asking how everybody was, how Rex the fox terrier was behaving, whether the Kansas City Blues were winning or losing . . . and then closed with this sentence: "I want to be a pastor."

On the following Thursday evening, I took the train home to Kansas City. My RLDS mother met me at Union Station the next morning, filled with excitement, approval, and curiosity about that concluding sentence of my postcard. Dad joined the conversation when he arrived home from work that Friday afternoon. The three of us sat in Pastor Weinhold's study at Immanuel Church in the early evening to share all this with him and to get his advice about where I should study for the ministry. I recall that he was pleased at the news of my call to the ministry and was immediately eager to recommend the school best suited for me among the choices of preparatory colleges in the Missouri Synod educational system. Although he was a board member of St. Paul's College in nearby Concordia, Missouri, he named St. John's College in Winfield, Kansas, as the best place for me to prepare for seminary. Knowing the version of interdenominational ecumenicity that prevailed in our home, as well as my public high-school education, which had offered neither Latin nor Greek, which were required for most Lutheran prep schools, he realized that St. John's was the better choice. There a more flexible academic administration would allow me to double up on Greek and Latin as well as build on the high-school German that I had enjoyed under a fine teacher (and fellow Immanuel parishioner), Alma Betz, at Paseo High School.

In little more than an hour's conversation in the cigar aroma of Pastor Weinhold's book-lined study, plans were laid that aimed me on a trajectory for the next nine years of my theological education. No one made a phone call to St. John's to inquire whether I might be accepted. No catalog of courses or bulletin with tuition and dormitory costs was available that evening. I didn't even know where Winfield, Kansas, was — and neither of my parents had ever heard of it. By nine that evening we were back home, putting all my gear in the small trunk Dad had brought home from his Marine Corps service in World War I. And by four o'clock the next morning we were chugging down Highway 50 in our '36 two-door Plymouth toward the southeast corner of Kansas.

By ten o'clock that Saturday morning, the blistering Kansas sun was already high and hot, causing several of the wartime tires of substitute rubber to develop noticeable goiters and the radiator system to throw up brownish-yellow water through the hood and onto the windshield. If my mother took this as a sign from heaven to turn back and keep her younger child at home, she did not say so. We waited under a large cottonwood until the shade and some water from a nearby farmhouse had cooled down the Plymouth enough for us to forge onward for the remaining seven hours of our ten-hour, 250-mile trek to Winfield.

What we found on the St. John's College campus was an administration and classroom building, the West Dormitory for men, the Baden Hall for women, and a small, cement-block building that housed the gymnasium. The student body numbered 400, mainly students from Lutheran families and congregations throughout the Midwest, with a few from as far west as California, and fewer still from east of the Mississippi. Our first stop on campus was the home of the president, whose name Pastor Weinhold had given us the night before. Dr. Edgar Mundinger got up from his dinner table to greet the three Luekings, who were, of course, total strangers to him. He cut an impressive figure, well over six feet tall and yet stocky, with a bushy head of hair, a strong face, an authoritative voice, and an unflappable manner. He did not blink when my father announced: "Here's Dean. He's our son. He'd like to be a Lutheran pastor. Can you take him?"

Dr. Mundinger looked me over for a couple of seconds in this pre-admissions examination at his front door, and concluded, "We'll give it a try." Then and there he introduced us briefly to Mrs. Mundinger, excused himself from the family at supper, and walked us over to West Dorm, where I was the thirteenth fellow to join a sleeping room of twelve who had moved in a week earlier. Classes had, in fact, already begun five days before I arrived. Most of my dozen instant roommates in this barracks-like arrangement of double-decker beds were just getting back from supper in the dining hall beneath the first floor of West Dorm. They greeted me with admirable warmth considering the circumstances — the arrival of a thirteenth guy in a "room" set up for twelve. I was shown the study desk I was to use in one of the two rooms across the hall, again jamming a seventh desk into an already crowded room for six.

With the domestic responsibility of finding me places to sleep and study taken care of, President Mundinger shook my hand, thanked my parents for depositing me in this new place for two years of my life, and returned to his supper table. On the way out, almost as an afterthought, he informed me that I should stop on Monday morning in his office to take care of such items as registration and the payment schedule for tuition, which was $400. My parents took this pell-mell arrival and acceptance in stride, in fact with something of a sigh of relief: within an hour or two I had been accepted into college, had been shown where to park my gear and where to study, and had met several friends whom I would value for a lifetime. Dad and Mom gave me a hug, got in the Plymouth, and drove back to Kansas City through the cool of the night rather than subject the tires and radiator system to another August midday of Kansas temperatures near 100 degrees.

This story of my call to ministry and admission into a small Lutheran junior college accentuates how simply and swiftly things unfolded in that one week in August 1945, which began with a Sunday spent in my uncle's alfalfa fields, with no clue in my mind about what I wanted to do with my future, and ended with my being a pre-seminary student in a school I had never heard of before. In my case, it was perhaps especially abrupt: the absence of ordained clergy in my family line tended to underscore the significance of my call to the ministry. It was not part of a well-tended plan in a family of pastors that would make it an obvious choice; rather, it came to me from outside. Behind the quotation at the head of this chapter (concerning the "have to" nature of being called to the ministry) can be a badgering by others to a forced decision that will surely backfire sooner or later; but something of the divine "must" does turn up often in St. Paul's letters. Motivation for ministry that begins with a clear sense that God is calling one to serve as an undershepherd has staying power when that shepherding must persevere through long, arid stretches. In the long-term pastorate the Spirit gave me, I had many occasions to return in memory to that mission festival in Lindenwood, Illinois, and draw sustenance from it for times of testing.

What a contrast between college admissions then and now! St. John's College was part of a pre-seminary Missouri Synod Lutheran system that had been adapted from Germany to America when the founders of the Missouri Synod migrated to Perry County, Missouri, in 1839. The first building they erected was a one-room log building for the purpose of preparing preachers. This German tradition was heavy on languages and humanities, without testing too thoroughly the extent to which the students who labored over Latin, Greek, and German were able to use those languages in preparation for seminary and the pastoral vocation afterward. The factor that lay behind President Carl Mundinger's on-the-spot acceptance of me, however, was not something of European origins. Rather, it was a product of the close-knit system of synodical connectedness. Carl Mundinger had known T. A. Weinhold at Concordia Seminary in St. Louis, where they had both studied; and though their paths parted when they graduated, they continued as members of a corps of clergy that was virtually a family. The Missouri Synod's major seminary in St. Louis, plus a smaller one in Springfield, Illinois, provided the four-year setting in which pre-seminarians from the Synod's eight feeder colleges formed bonds of collegiality and mutual awareness (and competition and clubbiness as well) that built a network of mutual acquaintance, if not trust, in all cases.

Thus, when I stood at the Mundinger door as one of Weinhold's parishioners from Immanuel in Kansas City, the signals enabling my acceptance on the spot went to work. In all likelihood, there was another factor involved beyond the force field of denominational connectedness: small junior colleges of the church always needed another name on the student roster with $400 more for the budget. I learned later that St. John's had a reputation for being more flexible than most of the other colleges in the system, due to the kind of creative leadership President Mundinger offered. He wrote the first critical history of the Missouri Synod (based on his doctoral dissertation at the University of Minnesota): it analyzed the factors behind the top-down system of governance in that church body.

Mundinger also brought together a faculty of outstanding individuals, given the size and location of the junior college. Foremost among them was Walter Wente, truly a Renaissance man with a Ph.D. from the University of Chicago, which he earned in record time following his seminary graduation. He had spent a year in Athens as a Daniel Shorey scholar in Greek language and classical literature and made the transition directly from Athens to Winfield to devote his exceptionally broad gifts as an educator to teaching New Testament Greek plus a smattering of Homer and other Greek classics to recent high-school graduates. He was both the academic dean of the college and a registrar who could size up nontraditional students like me quickly and organize a meaningful study program. With his wife, Pauline, as accompanist, Wente directed the college choir and bounced around the country roads of Kansas, Nebraska, and Oklahoma in the college bus, offering excellence in choral music to Lutheran congregations whose parishioners would then feed and house the Wentes and choristers overnight. His even greater musical service to the school was conducting the all-student-body polyhymnia for a December concert of Handel's *Messiah* in a congregation in Wichita, plus a springtime presentation of *Elijah*. There were

American colleges, large and small, that could boast of greater musical excellence in performing; but I have difficulty thinking of any whose director had more commitment to giving students a chance to learn music of lasting quality, with the only requirement of students from every kind of background being that they show up, rehearse faithfully, and sing to the best of their abilities.

Other professors served me well at St. John's, but Wente made the difference between a mediocre junior college tour through pre-seminary subjects and two years of genuinely valuable learning that served to whet my appetite not only for the seminary years ahead but for a lifetime of continuing to learn. This is what Walter Wente himself exemplified. With his positive example pressed on me from the first hour of my first day of classes at St. John's, I was gaining a major foundation stone for a long-term pastorate: growing in mind and soul through forty-four years rather than repeating one year's worth forty-four times over in a stagnation that suffocates both mind and soul.

Friendships formed at St. John's helped make my two years a happily fulfilling time. Ralph Phipps was among the first to welcome me to the sleeping "barracks." His subsequent vocation as a missionary in Japan and later as my colleague in a denominational battle broadened and deepened our ties and enriched my ministry in ways I could not have envisioned when we became classmates. Ken Behnken and Luther Roehrs were both classmates and teammates on the baseball team that did surprisingly well in spite of the limited size of our student body. St. John's had enough students from Oklahoma and Texas — which, I'm convinced, were hatching grounds for great ballplayers — to excel against much larger schools.

I was a southpaw pitcher, and in one of the last games I played before graduating, I had a good day on the mound against a college team in Lawrence, Kansas. After the game, a stranger came up and introduced himself as a scout for the Philadelphia Phillies; he asked whether I might be interested in talking over the possibility of joining their farm team in Salina, Kansas. The very idea of that prospect gave me a bigger hat size. But on more sober reflection, I realized that I did not want to leave Concordia Seminary before classes ended in the spring and return after they had started in the fall. Perhaps more to the point, I was realistic enough to know that I did not have the stuff that Robin Roberts and Curt Simmons had, both premier pitchers for the Phillies at the time. So I turned the Minor League contract idea down. Years later, however, I told this story in an article I wrote about why I liked my job as a pastor, mentioning that I was no Robin Roberts, etc. A few months after the article appeared, I received a letter from Robin Roberts, who by that time was a baseball coach at a Florida university. He thanked me for my complimentary remarks about his Hall of Fame pitching career, then mentioned that he had once given thought to going into the ministry but had moved on in baseball instead. Our sharing of experiences was like two trains passing in the night. To this day, however, when I walk into Wrigley Field or Comiskey Park in Chicago, I feel the flutter of a lingering question: What if . . . ?

My four years of study at Concordia Seminary in St. Louis, plus three years of vicarage, were spread out over what I now recognize as a prime time at that seminary. I could not have had better teachers than Richard Caemmerer, who made homiletics come alive in essential New Testament theology, as well as courses in the basics of writing and preaching a sermon. Paul Bretscher and Martin Franzmann provided New Testament courses that amplified the gospel-centered exegesis that avoided the twin pitfalls of fundamentalism and liberalism, which had created such a theological vacuum in the mid-1950s. Arthur Carl Piepkorn and Jaroslav Pelikan joined the Concordia faculty during my time there, and my study under both these scholars shaped my commitment to theology as a discipline of today's church as well as an awareness of the early church fathers and the development of doctrine through the centuries. Paul Bretscher's meticulous care as a teacher of philosophy and theology gave me a lifelong model to follow.

Caemmerer's genius for making preaching and theology genuinely inspirational — I remember the eagerness with which I anticipated his lectures — also contributed the central biblical image for the pastoral vocation that has guided me through all my years since. It is that of the pastor as equipper of the "saints," St. Paul's standard term for baptized believers. The key passage is Ephesians 4:11-13, with its testimony to God's gift of some to be prophets, pastors, teachers, and so forth, in order to prepare God's people for their daily ministry in the world. Embedded in that abundant passage is the gospel of Jesus Christ as the centering dynamic of all ministry; the pastoral vocation as God's gift rather than a human creation; a collegiality with other men and women who are called to other offices in the church; and the purpose of gospel, pastorate, and collegiality as the mission of the laity in the daily life of the world. The pastor as one who equips for ministry means so much to me because, down deep, I wondered how I could preach, teach, and serve the same congregation over many years by always staying one jump ahead of the faithful. That was my understanding of preaching: not feeding Christ's flock with the Bread of Life that his cross and resurrection offer, but serving up the thin gruel of my own latest insights or experience. Caemmerer turned that notion on its head, helping me to see the pastor as a servant of the Word rather than a track star well out ahead of the rest of the runners week after week. I was to deepen in the blessing of Ephesians 4 over the coming years of pastoral ministry at Grace Church, finding it to be the unchanging base that has meant both continuity and creativity for my calling. Discovering the solidity of that base during the years from 1954 until 1998 has been no small blessing. It is the backbone of my long-term pastorate.

Not everything was sweetness and light at Concordia Seminary in the late 1940s and early '50s. Some professors, especially those in dogmatics and Luther studies, had considerable talents for making vital truths of the faith insufferably dull, their lectures droning on and on about the obvious or the irrelevant. Our early student forays into inter-Lutheran contact with other seminarians did not fare well under a synodical administration that was nervous about such things. Our seminary chorus sang an anthem proclaiming on a high C that Christ has made us free, free, free! But we were not allowed to join in prayer with seminary students of the other major branches of American Lutheranism. That was a sign on the horizon of battles to come. For over a hundred years, the faculty of Concordia Seminary had handed down the last word on theological and pastoral issues among Missouri Synod clergy. It had been the undeclared teaching authority of a church body steeped in the authority of the congregation. What was causing that to unravel was the lessening of open disclosure by the faculty to the ministerium of the Synod that necessary changes in theology and church relationships were indeed taking place. That breakdown in communication stirred suspicion instead of trust, hostility instead of teachableness in too many clergy who did not take the time or effort to truly listen to the increasingly genuine confessional and biblical theology students were learning at Concordia Seminary. But these rifts were almost indiscernible throughout my seminary years in St. Louis. I did not dream then of the wrenching effect that breach, as it widened, would have on the seminary, the church, and the ministries of pastors throughout the land — including my own.

Between my second and third years of seminary, I vicared (i.e., interned) for a year as a member of the St. John's faculty at the highschool level and enjoyed teaching religion and English, as well as coaching boys' and girls' basketball. It was a taste of the teaching ministry, and it left me with an openness to the possibility of a teaching vocation in the future. In the summer of 1950, immediately following my vicarage year at St. John's, I spent three months in Mainz-Kastel, Germany, where I joined several dozen European youth in a World Council of Churches–sponsored work camp. We lived in tents just up from the banks of the Rhine and worked together in building a dormitory for East German refugee youths who were coming west in increasing numbers before the Berlin Wall went up. This was my first time outside the United States and began my acquaintance with Horst Symanowski, the pioneering German pastor in nonstipendiary pastoral ministry who also served as camp director. Some of the guest speakers he brought in told remarkable stories of their resistance activities in Germany and France during the Nazi years. Evening after evening we had our minds opened to the magnitude of the World War II horrors suffered by Jews and all who stood up against the darkest forces of the century. While hearing about the ghastliness of war from those who had experienced it firsthand, we could look across the Rhine to Mainz, still 85 percent destroyed five years after the war ended, with its French occupying force none too eager to rebuild the ruined city. I had experienced World War II only as a high-school student reading news stories and seeing newsreels at the Rockhill Theater near our house. It was a profound shock to live for a few months among those who had survived it.

That summer opened my mind to the pull of travel overseas. I had always been curious about our German relatives; we Luekings had been out of touch with them, except for occasional letters, since my grandparents had emigrated in the early 1880s. Following the work camp weeks, I took the train north to Luebbecke, near the village of Blasheim, where we still had cousins. My great-uncle, Wilhelm Maschmeier, was at the head of the welcoming party who met me at the train station, pipe in mouth, feet clad in wooden shoes, black cap doffed in my honor as he greeted me in the Low German dialect that was unlike anything I had learned in Alma Betz's high-school German class. It was a reunion of family ties that was understandably stiff at first; but it warmed up into a memorable visit, the first of several that would follow in later years.

Of much greater importance in opening me to the world was the two-year vicarage I spent in Japan between my third and fourth years of seminary. In the early spring of 1951, Dean Leonard Wueffel announced that the newly begun Missouri Synod mission in Japan needed six vicars to do work in English so that missionaries could have more time for language study. A group of third-year seminarians showed interest, and six of us were chosen. By late July we were on board a freighter bound from Seattle to Yokohama. We were met by William Danker, the mission leader, and a number of other missionaries under whom we were to serve. At something of a sorting-out session on the day of our arrival, I felt interest and admiration for all the missionaries there — except one. He was the one, of course, to whom I was assigned. What had turned me off during the introductory comments by this missionary was the superior attitude toward the Japanese that seemed implicit in his remarks. At least I took it as such, and I felt my heart sink when my name was placed with his in the vicar-missionary matchups. That first night in an upstairs bedroom of the missionary's home was sleepless as I began to think how long two years might be under these circumstances.

As it turned out, I learned more about getting along with people I had not chosen than I bargained for. It helped when I teamed up with Don Becker as a roommate after a few weeks. Later on, living in a Japanese home where no one spoke English put me much closer to the Japan I was eager to experience, including regular visits to the local bathhouse, where little boys would stare at my legs, longer and hairier than any they had ever seen. My vicarage assignment broadened out to a include partnership with Yoichi Imanari, a young Japanese interpreter with whom I began a Bible class in the home of Yoshie Ohta and her family in the Yokohama suburb of Ofuna. My first Sunday evening in Japan included a visit to the Yokohama Youth Fellowship, where I met Takuri Tei and heard him speak rather effectively on why he was not a Christian. I formed a friendship with him that brought us together on many evenings in his tiny room beneath an overhead railroad line in the dock section of Yokohama. He was born in what is now North Korea, came to Japan for a high-school education, and was caught in Tokyo during the war by restrictions that did not allow his return.

Reading the Gospel of Luke as Christmas approached in 1951, we came to the fourteenth chapter, where Jesus gives a unique proposal for whom to invite to dinner. Tei asked me if I had any problem with inviting the poor and outcast, those who could never repay the invitation, to a Christmas gathering. I had none, and we hosted just the kind of people Jesus had in mind as we prepared a sukiyaki feast on Christmas morning of 1951. Many of the stevedores living in houseboats and Japanese army amputees who lived under bridges, plus homeless waifs who roamed the dock area, belonging to no one, returned on December 26 for an encore after the Christmas Day banquet. That experience put Takuri Tei on a path of more serious inquiry into the Good News of Jesus' kingdom. He accompanied me and translated as I conducted Bible classes on houseboats, in jails, among courthouse judges, and in a vacation Bible school for children in Ofuna. He was baptized there in the summer of 1952, in an outside service under a large canvas tent that, unbeknownst to us, sported an advertisement for Kirin Beer in large letters on its roof. Later, Tei-san came to Kansas City to become a part of the Lueking family and study at the University of Kansas City. After a brief stint at Concordia Seminary, St. Louis, he became a proficient tax accountant, married a beautiful German-born woman, Madeline, and to this day is like a brother to me.

The Japan years profoundly shaped my outlook on ministry, giving me a global sense of the gospel and the church that have become part and parcel of my years in the Grace pastorate. I returned home from Japan the long way around, visiting churches and seminaries in Hong Kong, Singapore, and Sri Lanka (where classmate Andrew Fritze was doing missionary work), then a stopover in Bombay and on to Cairo and the Holy Land. In each place I sought to absorb some impressions that would become building blocks for future visits to these places. My partner in travel was Roy Schoeder, fellow seminarian and also a Japan vicar. Our destination in that summer of 1953 was Mainz-Kastel: we wanted to continue work there on housing for refugees — in the company of a new group of youths from Europe and Asia.

I was ready at last for my fourth and final year of theological study at Concordia Seminary when the fall of 1953 arrived. And although in matriculation I was out of step with many classmates with whom I had begun in 1947, one friendship begun that year had grown steadily through rooming together and the letters we exchanged during my sojourn in Japan. Martin Marty and I had come to the seminary from different preparatory colleges, and after meeting one day in the seminary quadrangle, decided it would be good to break up the prep school clubbiness that was too confining to both of us. We roomed together during our second year, deepening the roots of a friendship that would have lifelong influence. That was the year in which, among other accomplishments, Marty helped mastermind the invention of a completely fictitious theologian named Franz Bibfeldt, who had been sadly neglected since his time of influence earlier in the century. The whole spoof had been concocted to put a student mirror to faculty foibles; one professor, especially, made the amusing error of pretending in class that he could agree with Bibfeldt to a certain extent, but not entirely in some of the obscure theologian's more radical stands. It livened up campus life at the seminary for several weeks, before President Louis Sieck put an end to Bibfeldt — or nearly so. Under Marty's guidance, the Bibfeldt legacy resurfaced in the mid-

1970s at the University of Chicago Divinity School, where it was an immediate sensation, leading to the almost-annual scholarly Bibfeldt lecture on April 1, complete with luncheon, formal presentations, and a published volume on Bibfeldt's theology that was featured in *The New York Times* — all consequences of an intellectual spoof perpetrated on a seminary campus sorely in need of livening up.

With a friend like Marty, skilled in both Bibfeldt and serious theological reflection on the Christian presence in American life, I felt well prepared for whatever future was out there. I was blessed beyond words to have grown up under parents who gave me my first and most lasting spiritual roots. My years at St. John's College were notable for furthering the formation of my faith life and extending the beginnings that had been well formed in the parish of my youth. My four years of theological study were peak years of continuity and creativity in the best Lutheran tradition; and I had tested that training during two additional years of vicarage in Japan in overwhelmingly non-Christian surroundings. I had had glimpses of a Germany that was just beginning to recover from the devastations it had both caused and suffered in Europe. I was twenty-six years old, empowered by a call from God to the pastoral vocation. I was ready to get out of the starting blocks and run the race, one that turned out to be more than I could desire or deserve.

CHAPTER 3

Apprentice Years, 1954-1963

On the Monday morning after my Ordination Day, as I was busy getting my new workspace organized, a phone call came through for me. As I picked up the receiver, I heard myself, as though in an alien voice, answer, "Pastor Lueking speaking." The fact that I recall that moment and space so vividly is a commentary on the force with which the term *pastor* resonates in the Lutheran tradition. Clergy are called Reverend, Father, Mister, Parson, Deacon, Doctor, and a perhaps a few other names better left unmentioned — but "Pastor" is the title of choice among most Lutherans. Its translation from the Latin, "shepherd," points more to the function than to the individual person who bears it. It possesses a certain formality, yet without airs. Hearing my voice say "Pastor" in front of my name gave me pause, for it evoked in me strong and positive emotions from earlier years, which I knew would take some getting used to.

I would soon learn that others, too, would not immediately associate it with the twenty-six-year-old I was at that time. Not long after my first day on the job at Grace, I was returning from an errand in the city, pushing my Volkswagen Bug a little too hard on Washington Boulevard. One of Chicago's finest pulled me over to the side of the street, and while writing out a traffic ticket, looked up from his pad and asked: "Anyway, fella, what's your line of work?" Dressed as I was in blue jeans, an old plaid shirt, and a ball cap, I drew myself up to the dignity of my newly acquired title and answered: "I am an ordained Lutheran *pastor*." His surprised, perhaps typically Chicago, response was, "Full time . . . ?" After that brief conversation, the new full-time assistant pastor of Grace Church drove on, slowly, a full-time speeding ticket in his plaid shirt pocket, musing over the image expectations that go with being called pastor.

To be completely accurate, I was not the new assistant pastor but the new assistant *to* the pastor. Otto Geiseman had preferred that designation when he had introduced this addition to the pastoral staff of the congregation six years before my time. His choice of title was an unambiguous statement that Grace Church had one pastor, not two, or one and a half. His firmly held views on this principle of parish administration, and the theology he brought to it, were not ones he had arbitrarily chosen with an authoritarian intent. He remembered only too well the rancorous, divisive congregation he had inherited when he assumed this pastorate nearly a third of a century earlier — and the exceptionally strong pastoral hand required to deal with the problems he faced. To an uninformed observer, "assistant to the pastor" may have appeared to be a title insisted on by an insecure boss. But in Geiseman's belief and practice, in fact, it signified that the buck stopped with him as the servant of Christ; *he* was charged with bringing peace and a new sense of mission to a church whose disarray had done in the three previous pastors. Seeing how he gave meaning to pastoral servanthood in our eight years of working together, I later made his principle my own, under different circumstances and in different times.

Pastoral assistance had become a necessity at Grace in the late 1940s. A parishioner with a better eye for that than Geiseman himself, Paul Weiss, who had done well in the wholesale floral business, proposed not only help for the pastor but a willingness to fund it. With the approval of the congregation, Geiseman devised a program that would bring a seminary graduate in for ordination and two years of practical experience in all phases of parish ministry — plus the encouragement to do graduate study. The idea was not welcomed at synodical leadership levels, chiefly because of the idea's novelty: an ordination to a term call of two years. Nowhere among the six thousand parishes of the Missouri

Synod was there anything like it. Furthermore, it took the cooperation of Concordia Seminary in St. Louis to select the candidate and assign him to Grace; all of this involved uncomfortable negotiating with Synod President John Behnken and his vice presidents, who were never completely at ease with Geiseman and Grace Church in any case. It had taken all the persuasion Pastor Geiseman and the people in River Forest could muster to outlast the opposition and put the program in place in 1946.

The first assistant to the pastor at Grace Church, James Manz, served for three years while he began graduate work at Chicago Lutheran Seminary; he subsequently went on to a long pastorate at historic First St. Paul's in Chicago, site of the founding of the Missouri Synod in 1847. Kenneth Breimeier was the second assistant, from 1950 until 1952, and he went on to complete his doctorate at Northwestern University and serve as a mission pastor in a Chicago suburb before joining the Concordia Seminary faculty in St. Louis. Martin Marty, the third assistant, was assigned to Grace in 1952 for "seasoning under a mature pastor" (Geiseman) instead of being sent to London for ministry among European refugees, as was originally planned. It was Marty's leading role in creating the legend of Lutheran theologian Franz Bibfeldt during his seminary years that got him the "punishment" of being the assistant at Grace for two years. Geiseman was delighted with Marty's harmless spoof of overly stuffy theological educators and made his two years at Grace foundational for doctoral studies in American church history at the University of Chicago, his mission pastorate for seven years in the new suburb of Elk Grove Village, and his many years of distinguished writing and teaching at the Divinity School that have spread the leaven of his genius nationwide. By the time I arrived at Grace in 1954, the program had proven its worth, and the grumblings had been largely put to rest.

The wording of my pastoral position never mattered to me as I swung into the work at Grace. My assignments included areas customarily given to the recently ordained seminary graduate: conducting Sunday service liturgy and preaching once a month, youth ministry, teaching religion to seventh graders at Grace School, leading Saturday morning confirmation classes for public-school children, calling on the sick and homebound of the parish, making mission calls in the neighborhood, and spending every Saturday — from 3 to 5 and 7 to 9 — receiving communion announcements from those intending to take communion the next day.

This last practice was a carryover of a Lutheran version of personal confession and absolution, something that Martin Luther had highly recommended in his catechetical and other writings, but which was already on the wane by the time I came to Grace in 1954. On an average Saturday, usually no more than several dozen would call or come to my open office door to hear a brief biblical passage and a pastoral comment on the Lord's Supper. And those members would not stay long; but even those few minutes of conversation helped me get to know them. Pastor Geiseman had informed me, somewhat apologetically, about this part of my work, and I recall his hopeful suggestion that after 9 p.m. on Saturday evenings "there was still a lot of time left for a young single fellow to socialize." He had little idea of what that could mean. Some months into my Saturday evening confessional duties at Grace, I became aware of the very strong aroma of perfume from outside my study door, usually wafting my way shortly before the hour of nine. A Concordia student stood there, waiting to be the last person to announce for Sunday communion attendance, and she was usually dressed in tennis shorts and a tight T-shirt. I never acted on my mentor's suggestion to socialize after communion announcements: the perfume alone would have put me under.

The September meeting of the Women's Society of Grace was my first appearance before a group that had been a mainstay of service, friendship, and financial support for many needs within and beyond the congregation. Only a small percentage of the women of the parish worked outside their homes in 1954. Therefore, the Fellowship Hall was almost filled with young mothers, women in their middle years (who filled most of the leadership positions), and grandmothers and widows who welcomed this monthly gathering because of the luncheon, the speaker, and reports on coming activities. The meeting always began with prayer and Scripture, which was led by a member, followed by a pastoral greeting. I was introduced by Frances Wetzel — "Frankie" to everyone — who was among the first of the many gifted Grace Church women whom I came to know and admire. She and her husband, Edmund, had adopted twin boys who had been abandoned at birth by their mother, to add to their family of two daughters. She handled her household with the same graceful efficiency with which she handled her duties as president of the Women's Society.

Frankie had a keen eye for anything I had not noticed, for example, a dangling button about to fall off my suitcoat. Her concluding sentence in introducing me at that first Women's Society meeting was, "If anyone has a needle and brown thread, the button about to fall off our new assistant pastor's suitcoat could use some repair." After I had concluded my remarks, and before luncheon was served, Gertrude Huxhold came up to me, introduced herself as the one with needle and thread, and invited me to stop by the Huxhold home whenever I had the chance. I had met part of the Huxhold family on the previous Saturday at the wedding of her daughter, Barbara, who was escorted down the aisle by her brother, Bill — both of them smiling and radiant for the wedding despite the death of their father, Bill Huxhold, Sr., only a few weeks before. Gertrude sewed on my loose button, served me a delicious supper when I came to visit, and offered to take me in as the occupant of their guest room if that idea appealed to me. I did move there later in the fall, sharing the Gertrude Huxhold hospitality with Art Simon of the Concordia College faculty and several other young bachelors. We all ate at the Huxhold table, and we filled an empty household with conversation, laughter, and a helping hand when it was needed. It was more than a place to eat and sleep: I learned something there of the grievous loss that the death of one's beloved spouse imposes on a person and the ways in which a congregation can become a healing community for that grief. Gertrude was like a mother to me, and until her death in 1984, our families grew ever closer and remain so to this day.

Living in the parish neighborhood helped me get out into the homes of parishioners, and especially to make mission calls on newcomers, which was a primary part of my job description. We subscribed to a

Welcome Service, which gave us the names, addresses, and church affiliation (if there was any) of those who were new in the neighborhood. I
called on those who reported themselves to be either Lutheran or with
no affiliation. The purpose of my calls was to invite Lutherans to transfer from their previous parishes, and for those with no affiliation to attend a worship service to get a sense of what we were about, and if further interest developed, to join an adult instruction that covered the
basics of Lutheran faith and practice over a series of ten Sunday morning hours. Some did, but most did not. These sessions were conducted
each fall and spring, and I recall a sense of considerable satisfaction
when the numbers attending would reach twenty, sometimes thirty.
When I made my calls, I learned to listen for what lay beneath the usual
litany of reasons people had for saying they believed in God but had no
connection to his people in a congregation. When I experienced the inevitable discouragements of the task, I took heart from Reinhold
Niebuhr's *Leaves from the Notebook of a Tamed Cynic,* in which he remembered circling the block before working up the courage to ring a
doorbell in the industrial Detroit neighborhood where he began as a
young pastor.

An obvious fact was dawning on me in these apprentice years, yet
one that I had not been trained to heed: it was that for a pastor to know
his congregation, he needed to know the surrounding community, with
its ethos and assumptions. Though our area had a predominantly white,
middle- and upper-middle-class population, there was some diversity —
in ways that were not racial. I called on the home of Paul Harvey, who
was already well on his way to becoming a nationally known radio jour-
nalist with a strong appeal to a WASP listenership. He received me
courteously, announced his Plymouth Brethren roots, and dismissed me
promptly from his River Forest mansion. Years later he would use his
coast-to-coast network of radio stations to speak disapprovingly of my
efforts to establish Grace Church as a Saturday night shelter for the
homeless.

On the other side, I called on young couples with babies and a mortgage, often having to dispel the notion that Grace was a silk-stocking
congregation with a bias toward the well-heeled. In these first years of

my ministry, there were only rare occasions of nonwhite people moving in, and the Grace congregation had yet to receive its first African-American or Asian member. Anton Lopez was our token Hispanic member; he had entered the congregation through the influence of his German-Lutheran spouse, Elsie.

My Sunday morning functions were clearly defined: I conducted the liturgy, prepared the prayers, read Scripture, and assisted in distributing Holy Communion at the chancel rail, where communicants came forward to kneel and receive. We celebrated the Eucharist once a month at the 8:30 and 11 a.m. services; otherwise, it was squeezed in between the morning services at 10:15 twice a month, and on the second Sunday of the month at the 4 p.m. vesper service. It was a commentary on the lesser place the Lord's Supper occupied in an era of primary emphasis on preaching, which Geiseman did with seasoned excellence three Sundays out of four each month. My custom was to arrive well before the 8:30 first service and, among other things, open the pulpit Bible to the text for the day. One Sunday I checked with him a half hour or so before the service to see whether his sermon was to be from a First or Second Corinthians text.

"My sermon?" he asked with astonishment. "Aren't you preaching today?" I assured him that this was one of his Sundays to preach. Without further ado, he took pen and paper in hand, outlined a sermon on the spot, and preached it with none but me the wiser for knowing its preparation time of twenty minutes. Afterward he apologized for the mix-up, then advised me to wait twenty-five or thirty years before doing what he did that Sunday. Pastor Geiseman was helpful in critiquing my pulpit work on occasion, but we had no regular schedule of sermon feedback. I was not unhappy with my schedule of infrequent preaching because my plate was full enough, since I started graduate studies at the Divinity School of the University of Chicago in the fall following my ordination.

I entered the pastoral ministry at Grace actively interested in the prospect of returning to Japan and the Far East for a missionary vocation, something that both Pastor Geiseman and the congregation knew well

44

before I accepted the call to Grace. The impact of my overseas vicarage years was shaping the initial direction of my graduate education; at the same time, I valued the projected two years of practical experience in a congregation such as Grace for whatever and wherever my future would be.

The University of Chicago Divinity School had two outstanding faculty members at that time who drew me there to broaden my base for understanding the Asian religious and cultural context, of which I knew little — only that I should learn more about both contexts and needed these two scholars for that purpose. One was Joachim Wach, a respected German theologian with an international reputation for his work in the broad phenomenon of religious life and practice across the spectrum of the world's religions, known as *Religionswissenschaft*. He impressed me first with his grasp of a subject that was new to me and, second, with the care he took in pausing in his lectures before choosing exactly the right English phrase for the German one that immediately came to his mind. He was generous in the time he gave me in consultations on my overall study goals, combining expertise with empathy in helping me design an academic program suitable for my vision of a possible missionary vocation in Japan. After some weeks of lecturing, he set me to translating some of his German writings to enlarge the bibliographical materials needed in a field that was not overcrowded with English titles.

The other scholar was Joseph Kitagawa, an American-born Japanese who had personally suffered through the disastrous years of our government's internment of Nisei Americans during World War II. Kitagawa was new at the Divinity School when I came to study there, but was quickly gaining favor with students, who responded well to his solid scholarship in Asian religion along with his quiet manner, subtle sense of humor, and genuine interest in each student. I began my course work with him by studying the field in which he was most noted, Hinayana Buddhism. It was an interesting and unique experience in my life: spending four of the five weekdays heavily involved in mission calls, ministry to the sick and aged, and teaching twelve-year-olds the catechism — and one day of the week in the radically different academic world of a non-Christian religion. This was neither an easy nor a natural mix, but I was content to believe that each of the two worlds somehow complemented and supplemented the other, although I was acutely aware of how inexperienced I was in both parish ministry and the academic study of religion.

My graduate work changed abruptly in the summer of 1955. Joachim Wach died suddenly while in Europe; and Joseph Kitagawa was soon to move from the classroom to become academic dean of the Divinity School. I took a course with Friedrich Heiler, another German who had come in Wach's place for a semester of teaching in the History of Religions Department. I was aware of his specialty because Wach had introduced me to his best-known work, *The Idea of the Holy,* the year before. While academically brilliant, Heiler was also the stereotypically eccentric German scholar who could not find his way back to the campus after getting lost in downtown Chicago. I could hardly count on him for mentoring me through the thicket of course work in the specialized field I had chosen. In short, I was floundering. I felt increasingly frustrated by the uncertainty of where I was called to go and of how God would guide me to whatever destination he had in mind.

In the spring of 1956, on a sunny day that was itself a sign of providence at work, I met Jaroslav Pelikan coming out of the door at Swift Hall as I was about to enter. Having studied historical theology under him at Concordia Seminary, I knew him well enough to request, when he asked how things were going, that he sit down with me for a conversation in the Swift Hall quadrangle. He heard my story, grasped my dilemma quickly, and made a suggestion that became another hinge on which my life and vocation turned. Why not concentrate on the sending side of the Christian mission rather than the receiving side? Given the uncertainty into which my study plans had fallen, it made sense instantly. A new addition to the Divinity School faculty, Robert Pierce Beaver, was the reigning expert among American scholars of mission history. Sidney Mead was second to none in his scholarly perception of the uniqueness of American Protestantism, the setting for the great missionary movements that spread out to the world from nineteenth-century America. And I already knew Jaroslav Pelikan as the established young Lutheran theologian and historian of both Lutheran and patristic development of doctrine, as well as knowledgeable in nearly everything else in church history. Within a half hour, a new direction for my graduate study emerged.

Once again, as in a rural Lutheran parish mission festival a decade before, an almost serendipitous occasion had come as an answer to my prayers. Jaroslav Pelikan became my chief doctoral study advisor, with Beaver and Mead as partners on the dissertation committee. Four years later, which included one year of full-time residency in graduate study at the University of Chicago, I received my Ph.D. degree. My dissertation was a historical study of mission motivation and method in the Missouri Synod at home and overseas, and it was later published as *Mission in the Making*. On a March day in 1960, as Chancellor Robert Hutchins handed me my diploma in the Gothic cavernousness of Rockefeller Chapel, a fellow graduate student reminded me, "Just remember, Lueking, Josef Goebbels had a Ph.D, too."

Jaroslav Pelikan and his wife, Sylvia, were instrumental in another serendipitous turning point in my life, this one of far greater magnitude. One late November day in 1956, they invited me to lunch at their Dorchester Avenue apartment, near the University. While enjoying the food and conversation, I picked up a saltshaker to season my food and noticed the words "Joseph Frano Hardware, Boyceville, Wisconsin" printed on the saltshaker. I made an offhand remark that I would like to meet Joseph Frano someday and thank him for a saltshaker that really salts. Sylvia Pelikan's eyes lit up at the comment. She explained that Joseph Frano was her new father-in-law: her widowed mother had married this widower, a fellow Slovak Lutheran, about a year before. Joseph had two daughters, she added, her voice warming to the idea in her mind, one married and one single. As it turned out, Beverly, the single daughter, a physical education teacher at Lincoln High School in Manitowoc, Wisconsin, was coming to visit the Pelikans. Sylvia asked whether I could possibly meet Beverly at the Northwestern Station in downtown Chicago, since the Pelikans were committed to a university function on the Friday night of her arrival. Not inclined to turn down a request from my faculty advisor's wife, I immediately said I would be glad to.

I did as promised, posting myself at the head of the arrival platform on that December 7 evening, looking for a physical education teacher named Beverly among the several hundred people getting off the train. One tall, slender young woman who was wearing a tan coat and a broad-brimmed hat did catch my eye; but I knew it could not be Beverly, because this person looked like no physical education teacher I had ever seen. In fact, she was a stunning contrast to my stereotype of physical education teachers — who would be of sturdy build, with muscular calves and severely bobbed hair, wearing tweedy wool suits and sensible shoes. Nevertheless, I walked up to this person who, I was sure, could not be the one I was to meet, announced who I was, and asked if by the wildest chance in the universe she might be Beverly Frano. She said that yes, she was Beverly Frano. Right then and there I said to myself, not to her, "I hope I can marry you." I escorted her to my Volkswagen Bug, which was parked outside the station, and we drove to the Tropical Hut on Fifty-fifth Street, near the University, where we sat conversing when the Pelikans walked in. Sylvia Pelikan took one look at us, me with my head propped up in my left hand as I sat in transfixed attention to Beverly, and shot me a glance as if to say: "Aha!" She read my mind exactly.

I did not ask Beverly to marry me on the spot. I waited a long time — just under four weeks — until after I had met her family in a visit to their northwestern Wisconsin home. Her answer to my ridiculously premature proposal was, "Do you know what you are talking about?" I answered, "Trust me," and she has been doing that for four and a half decades since. We were married eight months later in the Slovak Lutheran Church of the Holy Trinity several miles outside Boyceville, Wisconsin. It was a kind of wedding cum pastoral conference: Otto Geiseman was the officiant, Jaroslav Pelikan the preacher, Martin Marty the best man, and my seminary friends Walter Bouman and Edward Schroeder were in the congregation, together with our families and friends, including my landlady, Gertrude Huxhold, who had hosted a bridal shower for Beverly prior to the wedding. Slovak wedding receptions are hardly possible without dancing, heavy on the polka tunes. Among the first things Beverly asked me when we began wedding plans was how ready I was to polka. I was ready.

Joseph Frano, my new father-in-law, had warned his daughter that marrying a preacher meant living out of the missionary barrel in all likelihood, which didn't seem to phase Beverly's willingness to make the best of whatever circumstances lay ahead for us. Our beginning in married life was a doubling of both of our vocations: she joined the faculty of Concordia College in River Forest as an instructor in physical education, while I finished writing my dissertation. A collective sigh of relief seemed to rise from the Grace Church parishioners as they welcomed Beverly to their hearts and to an active role in the life of the congregation, which grew in breadth and depth as the decades unfolded. I continue to marvel at the abundance and sturdiness of our marriage that was a result of a proposal made and accepted within a month of meeting each other. I can account for it only as a sign of great grace from God, who had heard from me often enough during my three bachelor years after ordination. My mother's delighted exclamation on first meeting Beverly summed it up well: "Son, you drove your ducks to the right pond!"

How much Beverly meant and still means as a pastor's spouse and partner in ministry is incalculable. Psalm 128 draws the picture that may not measure up to the many-faceted role of today's woman, but the image of a wife as a fruitful vine within the house and children as olive plants around the table still speaks a benediction that is deep and lasting. Olive plants around our table appeared one by one during those apprentice years of our family life: first Ann in 1960, then Christopher a year and a half later, followed by Sarah in 1968 and Joel in 1970. The circle of our immediate family grew during those years because of our temporary foster care of babies waiting for permanent adoption via the nearby Lutheran Child and Family Services. It was good for us and for our children to share the blessings of our home with infants and toddlers who had none. Over thirty infants came into our care as our own children were growing up. One six-year-old lad, Tim Lovell, was a part of our family for three years before his mother could care for him again.

We Luekings formed a strong bond with him as he experienced the ups and downs of life in the parsonage. His own family had known rocky times beyond anything we could imagine, and it was good for us and our children to gain some sense of what many children suffer in homes of lovelessness and violence. One of Tim's older brothers had disappeared one day. At long last, police were able to identify his body as one of the twenty-eight boys unearthed from the crawl space of John Wayne Gacey's house on Chicago's north side. Tragedies of that magnitude were sobering reminders to our family of the terror that strikes by noonday in a dangerous world, distant from the reconciling mercies of God and his Son, who came to take on those terrors firsthand as victor through a bloody cross.

Our family circle also grew from time to time from unexpected events in the course of pastoral ministry. One evening two police officers knocked on our door with a seventh grader from our school standing between them. Joni Babikian had finally worked up enough nerve to seek police help in dealing with her alcoholic mother, who kept Joni up long past a child's bedtime to mix the gin and vodka drinks after she was too drunk to do so herself. As a result, Joni would arrive at Grace School late and exhausted from lack of sleep on too many school mornings. She was an only child, bright and already streetwise beyond her twelve years. She had asked the police to take her to our home so that she might "stay a couple of nights" — until things got straightened out at home.

This was an arrangement that probably should have been directed through the proper family service agencies, which are more experienced than we were in these matters of major responsibility. But whatever the risks were, anything was better than allowing an intolerable home situation to go on unattended. The real help, of course, was needed by Joni's mother. Her father had left the family years before (I don't recall having ever seen him), and Grace School teachers and student friends provided the main stability in life for Joni, who needed so much and asked so little. She stayed with us for several months; her mother was more than willing to keep her in our care and indulge her alcoholism unimpeded. This arrangement, tailor-made for codependency, was brought to and end, however, when both Vic Waldschmidt, the Grace principal, and I made it clear that either she would have to resume her parental care or Joni would have to enter into the labyrinth of the Illinois Department of Child Care for foster family placement. We avoided that blight as we did our best to monitor the ⌐ome situation. Mrs. Babikian moved away with Joni after she graduated, but I still picture that resolute, frightened child standing between two policemen at our parsonage door, and I can't help wondering how her life has gone since she was a part of our family and parish school community.

On another occasion I was called to the family court as a witness to problems encountered in another Grace School family. This time the judge sent *three* children home with me until some more permanent determination concerning their future could be made. The first evening they moved in, one escaped by jumping off the low roof outside our guest bedroom door; it took me several hours of driving around the neighborhood to find him. It was no help to Beverly that the children's mother would often come for a visit shortly before our family's supper hour, filling the kids with cake and cookies that spoiled their appetites for our family meal. The two boys and their sister were with us for several months before the family dissolved because of their parents' divorce; the children faced a future that was as unpromising as the indifference on their father's face, the anger on their mother's.

A happier outcome of our expanded family began with Sophie Jimenez's entry into our congregation and our lives. She had come from Mexico as a single mother of three, the youngest of whom, Philip, was a Grace School classmate of our youngest child, Joel. Sophie had built up from scratch a successful hair salon business in downtown Chicago; her schedule meant working late on Thursdays. She asked if Philip might become our Thursday child after school, which began a friendship that has deepened to this day, making us like family to each other. Sophie has cut my hair for years as part of a regular supper visit ritual, and early on she sized up my receding hairline as a likely site for the hairpieces she makes. I always demurred, claiming that I had enough to do taking care of what was in my head to worry about what was or wasn't on top of it. But one day Sophie arrived for supper with a radiant smile, her hands clasped in happy anticipation of my improved appearance as she presented me with a hairpiece that fit the empty space perfectly. I thanked her profusely, and then tried it on amidst hoots of laughter and general derision by all in our household. I put it in a drawer, where it stayed for several years, until the occasion arrived for the one and only time I wore it. That was the day after a wedding I conducted for my niece in Seattle. At the end of my day with the family, I asked my sister, Donnis, if she noticed anything different about her brother. "Of course I did," she answered, "but I didn't want to embarrass you by saying how funny you looked." Never again did I have the nerve, nor the desire, to show up in the pulpit more generously thatched than I am naturally via Sophie's handiwork, even when I later learned the exorbitant cost of these tributes to male vanity — and thus the value of Sophie's gift.

Both Beverly and I had come from families with open doors to relatives, friends, and those down on their luck. As we were establishing our roots within our own family, opening the doors to others for shorter or longer periods of time was something we found natural. It reached beyond foster babies and Grace School children to include several dozen foreign students as our children were growing up. Hiroko was with us for two years as a graduate student in organ and church music at Concordia College. She was the older daughter in the Ohta family of Ofuna, Japan, a family who had opened their home to me ten years earlier for a Bible class that led to the formation of a congregation and a kindergarten that numbers several hundred children today. Since her stay we have had students living with us from Spain, Argentina, Syria, Hong Kong, Switzerland, and Austria. Sharing hospitality, expressed in the Benedictine blessing engraved on our front door knocker, "Let all guests be received as Christ," was a ministry of our family with Beverly at its center. She made the welcoming cheerful, did the extra work with a flair and without complaint, and has won a permanent place of affection and respect in the hearts of those who have come — and still come — from near and far.

With the completion of my doctorate in the spring of 1960, I returned to full-time pastoral work at Grace Church. Otto Geiseman was 67, and I was 32. With the future ministry at Grace on his mind, he began discussions with Grace leaders and me about his vision for pastoral succession. I would be called as an associate pastor and over the next several years would assume an increasing share of the work, while his part would gradually lessen until his seventieth year, when he would retire. I would then become the senior pastor. This plan stated clearly that he and Marie would remain in the parsonage after that, and he would continue on in occasional pastoral assignments; it had no particulars on the nature and extent of such a continuing ministry. His concept of a workable future defied every maxim of what has become the received wisdom on successful pastoral transitions, especially when an exceptionally strong, gifted, and still-present leader hands over the reins after forty years of service. On the surface it looked like a sure-fire formula for mutual frustration and inevitable conflict, a recipe for the failure of a congregation and its new pastor to flourish with innovative programs as well as keeping continuity with the Grace tradition of gospel-centered ministry.

We were not naïve about these obvious pitfalls, and we discussed them candidly. Geiseman's goal, I truly felt, was not padding his own future in a self-serving fashion. He spoke of a continued working relationship, bringing forth the best each could offer for the good of the parish. He knew enough horror stories of pastors who bedeviled their successors with meddling and undermining; but he did not regard our warmly collegial partnership to be so fated. We had worked together without any major rift for six years. Could it continue with mutual benefit under new circumstances? Could he really let go? Could I truly lead with this strong, capable man, who had taught me so much and whom I genuinely respected and loved, looking over my shoulder?

Whatever the odds were for or against that vision, I accepted the call issued by the congregation to become the associate pastor and entered its full-time work when I had completed my graduate work in 1960. No sooner were we on our way in a deeper and broader bond of mutual ministry than everything was thrown awry by a development as unwelcome as it was unexpected: Otto Geiseman was diagnosed with lung cancer. He gave me the news in a conversation I shall not forget. He asked me to sit down with him in his study, and I knew from his tone and demeanor that something serious was at hand. He pointed to his right side and spoke of a pain there "like a wire cage under my ribs jabbing me with a hundred sharp edges." Robert Sharer, a parishioner and a thoracic surgeon, had ordered exploratory surgery immediately. He would be sidelined for months, Geiseman said, with the ultimate outcome known to God alone. Looking me steadily in the eye, he asked me to accept the immediate and full responsibility of the pastoral care of the congregation and its staff of two dozen. Shocked though I was by the news, I tried to put into words the wobbly feelings rushing over me as I pledged my readiness to do what needed doing.

Geiseman's surgery revealed that the resected cancerous mass was malignant. This would mean months of prolonged chemotherapy treatment for him; for me it meant a sudden, unasked-for plunge into the full range of pastoring the congregation. In those spring and early summer months of 1960, I experienced for the first time in my pastoral life the discipline of preaching every Sunday; teaching adults and youth who were preparing for confirmation; attending to the sick, aged, and troubled souls of the parish; assuming the administrative duties of regular meetings with the elders; and presiding at the monthly meetings of the church council. Richard Gotsch, already two years along as pastoral assistant before Geiseman's illness, accepted a third year of service at Grace and was immensely helpful. But with the key pastoral figure absent and seriously ill, I learned firsthand one of the qualifications for ministry that is not teachable in seminaries, what St. Paul accepted as "the daily pressure of my anxiety for all the churches." However, it did not occur to me to seek further pastoral help for the daily work; there was too much uncertainty about Pastor Geiseman's recovery — whether and when and to what extent. Minister of Music Paul Bouman and Grace School Principal Vic Waldschmidt, always collegial since my first day at Grace, became even more valued as supportive partners in my now expanding role as de facto pastor of the congregation. Above all, the people of Grace expressed their confidence in God's leading by accepting my preaching, teaching, and administering with grace and patience.

To the relief and gratitude of us all, Pastor Geiseman did recover.

54

He recovered well enough, in fact, for the church council to endorse an idea that had been on my mind during the months of his convalescence. He had close pastoral friends in missionary posts around the world, and I knew they would cherish a visit from him. He had developed a series of lectures on the ministry of St. Paul and was ready to offer the best of his pastoral years as a commentary on the great apostle's ministry. I wrote to colleagues in Japan, Korea, Hong Kong, Sri Lanka, India, the Holy Land, and Europe, outlining an itinerary for the Geisemans and suggesting the mutual value of a visit to each place. Not many clergy in 1960, just recovered from cancer surgery, circled the globe to listen and learn and to give the best of the seasoned pastoral wisdom they had gained from decades of congregation-based ministry.

The Geisemans eagerly accepted the plan once he had received the green light from his doctor. As a celebration of the providence of God in his recovery, the church held a parish-wide banquet in the Concordia College gymnasium as a send-off for their global journey of several months. Arthur Wellman, chair of the elders, declared Dr. Geiseman "The Ambassador from Grace" as he presented him with a leather briefcase that held the air tickets and arrangements at each stop along the way. All went well, abroad and at home, and Geiseman wrote often about his varied adventures. A typical report to the parish — this one sent from Hong Kong with details of meetings with pastors and seminary faculty — included his fascination with a Chinese jazz band in a night club to which the Geisemans' hosts had taken them. In a vintage Geiseman comment, he said that if he could preach like the drummer could pound out the jazz beat, he would be getting somewhere. His stay in India was especially meaningful: his spiritual kinsman of many years, Luther Meinzen, hosted him for a week with the Concordia Seminary faculty and pastors of surrounding congregations of Nagercoil, India, at the southernmost tip of the subcontinent.

His return in the fall of 1960 was a joyful and hopeful resumption of our partnership as we began in earnest to put the transition plan into action. In the summer of 1961 that partnership was tested when I was called by the Board of Foreign Missions of the Missouri Synod to teach in the Lutheran Seminary in Tokyo, Japan. Beverly and I shared that information with Geiseman and the congregation, of course, and gave it full consideration because I had not dismissed it from my mind during the eight years since my return from vicarage in Japan. In August a special meeting of the Voters' Assembly was called to deliberate the matter. I spoke of my growing sense that in Japan the teaching of seminarians should be done by Japanese rather than Americans; and I spoke as well about my more basic conviction — that my primary calling was to the parish rather than the classroom. The response to me was a request to stay with the Grace program of transition, which I did.

What was not said — but felt by all — was the question of Pastor Geiseman's health as he looked forward to easing his schedule in the two years before his formal retirement. That concern returned to the forefront shortly after Christmas, when, early in 1962, the cancer returned. This time the surgery revealed the metastasized disease as incurable. Dr. Sharer informed him that he had no more than a few months to live. Pastor Geiseman accepted it, but not without a monumental battle. Throughout the spring and summer of 1962, he spent the majority of each day stretched out on the couch in the parsonage's living room, battling the demons that assault a dying man with so much to live for. In September, his weakened condition meant a return to West Suburban Hospital. No sooner had he entered the hospital than Felix Gutgesell, Grace Church's janitor since the 1930s, died on the job of a massive heart attack. Geiseman's comment, "So, Felix beat me to eternity, didn't he?" expressed what was on his mind and helped me understand that Christians approaching death often view everything in the perspective of eternity — *sub specie aeternitatis,* as our forebears of previous centuries put it.

With his energies depleted day by day, Geiseman asked less about people and events in the congregation and chose not to receive many visitors besides his family and me. At first this puzzled me. Why, after ministering to so many people in their final days, would he not welcome the ministry of the many who wanted to see him and make their supportive love known to him in a personal visit? On further reflection, though, I came to realize that he needed all his energies just to make it from one day to the next in his long, slow slide into weakness and death.

At no point, however, did he express bitterness against God for this crushing blow to his hopes for a good transition and retirement into writing and speaking, a lighter pastoral load, travel, and unencumbered time with his family, something so long denied by the demands of the earlier years. He dictated no pastoral letter to the congregation expressing the concern and affection he felt for them; instead, he left it to me to keep the people informed. The one communication he asked me to make was that the children of the parish "storm the gates of heaven in my behalf" as he put it, begging God for deliverance to a longer life, but in any case asking for their prayers that God's will be done. After two months in the hospital, when his death was imminent, he opened the subject of his funeral for the first time. He asked me to preach the sermon, using as the text the Third Petition of the Lord's Prayer, that God's will be done on earth as in heaven. It touched me deeply that he asked me to be the preacher, since there were so many others who could and would have served readily and with distinction. He emphasized, however, that his funeral was no occasion for distinguished preachers. What counted, as I recall him saying in quiet resignation, was that Christ was exalted, "since he will be their only refuge and strength when our people come finally to where I am now."

He slipped into a coma and died on November 7, 1962. I received the news from parish secretary Clara Christopher while in the middle of a pastoral message to the Women's Society in Fellowship Hall. I drove immediately to West Suburban Hospital in the chill and drizzle of a bleak November afternoon, the weather matching my mood as I prepared to minister to the family and the parish in the hours immediately ahead. The church followed an unusual old custom for the twenty-four hours prior to his funeral: his body lay in state in the sanctuary where he had so often preached the good news of One who had robbed death of its sting. As symbols of the close pastor-parishioner ties over four decades of his ministry, two honor guards flanked his casket, changing at hourly intervals, as hundreds of people came to comfort the family and say good-bye to their pastor. I preached the Matthew 6 text at the funeral service, as he had requested. The Grace choirs, adult and children, sang. Missouri Synod President Oliver Harms spoke a tribute on behalf of the larger church. And the people prayed in thanksgiving for a pastor deeply loved over several generations. Thus ended the Geiseman era of forty abundant, eventful years, the last eight of which I had the privilege of sharing with him in the Grace pastorate.

Caring for the congregation as well as for Pastor Geiseman through most of 1962 was a prime time of pastoral apprenticeship for me in new and deeper dimensions. The daily visits to the hospital bed of the man who had shaped my pastoral formation more than any other taught me that pastors, too, must finally hurl against the obscenity of death — this time their own death — the foolishness of the gospel they have preached for a lifetime to others: a cross, a crucified rabbi, a grave with no body in it, a wild rumor started by hysterical women, and then the regal command of a King, "Put your hands in my wounds, see my hands, it is I!" Among the many tributes paid to Otto Geiseman, none caught the quintessential pastoral essence of him better than the one that appeared in *The Cresset,* a Valparaiso University publication of which he was a founder and editorial associate for seventeen years. It was probably his longtime friend and soul mate in many a church cause, President O. P. Kretzmann, who wrote the unsigned editorial salute:

> Geise was one of the most rambunctious members of a rambunctious generation of churchmen. He could be kind as few men could be kind, but whenever he found the Word bound by any human obstacles to its free course, his instinctive reaction was to reach for the meat-axe. . . . But the gallant fighter was, more than anything else, a dedicated pastor. In the quiet of his study he could be the most patient and understanding of men. In the face of human sin and frailty he was unshockable for, like his Lord, he knew what was in the heart of man and he was ready to take men as he found them. But he was never content to leave them where he found them. The grace of God which he offered to those who came to him with their problems was always free, but never cheap. And he did not waste his time on those who were looking for painless cures. But among the many who mourn his passing are hundreds who, by reason of him, went away and believed on Jesus. . . .

I took these words as more than a eulogy to the Geiseman past. They were to me a summons to the future of a rich and daunting pastoral tradition now handed on to me. My years of apprenticeship were over, my educational tools were in hand, and my spouse and young family were with me. As I would learn sooner than I had anticipated, the promise as well as the perils of the pastoral office at Grace Church would carry me into a future that was new and indeed rambunctious in ways beyond my knowing.

CHAPTER 4

Becoming the Pastor

*The minister becomes, in effect, a chaplain to the parish as
a whole, but a pastor only to those who want to be serious
about their Christian profession. . . .*

JAROSLAV PELIKAN

Since they had not called a pastor in forty years, it was a new experience
for Grace Church in late 1962 to learn how it is done. In our branch of
Lutheranism, heir of a strong denominational heritage of congregational autonomy, the initiative for and leadership in the process was
strongly congregation-centered. By December 1962, the church had
formed a Call Committee, with Dewey Carlson as chairman. The Grace
situation was somewhat unusual, since the call they had made to me in
1960 to become the associate pastor included the transition plan
whereby I would become the senior pastor on Dr. Geiseman's retirement. That automatic succession seemed unwise to me as the parish
prepared to make a decision of such magnitude. And so, when that subject was reviewed by the elders and the Voters' Assembly, and Arthur
Wellman made the proposal for an open slate (he had talked it over with
me privately beforehand), I was all for it.

By February 1963, five new names had been added to mine on the slate: Kenneth Breimeier, William Bruening, Richard Gotsch, William Kohn, and Martin Marty. In March, a letter to the membership from the Call Committee announced its decision to put forward my name as its choice. The Call meeting took place in the sanctuary on April 2, with men only attending and voting (this was 1963; women's suffrage would not come to Grace Church until 1970). After the meeting opened, I gave a brief pastoral report on other matters, and then went home to help Laurie Nelson babysit our Ann and Chris. About nine o'clock, Louis Menking called to inform me that I was the newly elected pastor of Grace Lutheran Church. While that outcome may have seemed obvious, it would have been presumptuous of me to take it for granted. I was humbled and moved by being called, and I was especially grateful that the call process had been open. Above all, I trusted that God was speaking through the decision of the congregation that evening.

The Installation Service was on the Sunday evening of April 28, 1963. I had asked that President Martin Koehneke of Concordia College preach, which he did with his gift of making the gospel news — truly good news. He and I had come to River Forest together in 1954, he to the college and I to Grace. From our first meeting we had become soul mates and collaborators in deepening the ties between parish and college as we worked together whenever possible during the following years. He and Irma and their family were active parishioners, respected by all and especially by me, a dozen or more years his junior but always lifted by his buoyant spirit, keen mind, and generous participation as a Grace parishioner. Koehneke's sermon, based on Romans 1:16 and entitled "Pastor Lueking, Meet Grace Church; Grace Church, Meet Pastor Lueking," called us to see the new thing Christ was doing, to take nothing for granted just because this pastor and parish had already known each other for a few years, and to keep the power of the gospel at the heart of the common ministry of college and church (Grace counted some fifty of the Concordia faculty and their families among its members). It was a thrilling evening for Beverly and me, and it buoyed us for the new era now beginning.

During the five weeknights prior to my installation, I had invited the membership for informal pastor-to-people conversations concerning my vision of where we were and whither we were heading. Many accepted that invitation, and the sight of Fellowship Hall well filled — with all of us sitting in a large circle — was a heartening symbol to me of the new relevance of the signature passage of my pastorate, the Ephesians 4:11-13 theme of equipping laity for daily ministry in the world. As a token of something new in a new era, I had asked Elfrieda Miller of the Grace School faculty to prepare tables filled with a variety of reading materials — devotional literature, newer Bible translations, and children's Bibles — for people to browse through while continuing conversations and drinking coffee. It was an effort to gather as many of the parish membership as possible to take stock of our strengths and weaknesses. Only six months had passed since the death of a much-loved and respected pastor for forty years; these five evenings of mutual conversation and consolation (a phrase from the Lutheran confessional writings) helped to heal and hearten us for an unknown future.

Events in the nation during 1963 added considerably to the unsettling sense that America was heading into stormy waters. During the week of my installation, Governor George Wallace had defied Attorney General Robert Kennedy's order for federal troops to quell race riots in Alabama. Martin Luther King and Ralph Abernathy led a civil rights march on the state capitol in Birmingham. In June, Medgar Evers was assassinated by a sniper in Jackson, Mississippi. In September, four little girls were killed during Sunday school by a bomb thrown into the window of a Negro church in Montgomery. And only two months later, the nation and world mourned the assassination of President Kennedy.

Two days after that national trauma, Americans recoiled at the television footage of Jack Ruby gunning down presidential assassin Lee Harvey Oswald. I remember Bill Tatman, on duty as an usher that Sunday morning, hurrying back to the sacristy with that news just as I was about to enter the chancel and begin the 11:00 service. Neither he nor I knew what to do with such information other than to add one more petition for our nation in the prayers of the day. Since the Cuban missile crisis of late October 1962, the children of Grace School had been trained in classroom drills to crouch under their desks in the event of a nuclear attack. Hardly a month went by in 1962 and 1963 without some new nation shaking off colonial rule in Africa and struggling into nationhood. The Roman Catholic Church felt the tremors of new times, as Pope John XXIII opened the Second Vatican Council in Rome and the winds of *aggiornamento* brought changes that unsettled many in the Catholic Church who preferred the Latin Mass, chancels unchanged, laity in the pew where they belonged, and priests maintaining a distance from racial and other social struggles. These were not tranquil times.

In August 1963, Martin Luther King issued a call for everyone committed to nonviolent solutions to the nation's increasingly violent racial problems to come to Washington, D.C., for a mass protest against the wrongs black Americans had suffered for over three centuries. I heard his appeal on an evening newscast and immediately told Beverly that I was going. Her response was a twofold request: the first was that I wear my clerical collar, which had not, however, been particularly protective of clergy who joined freedom riders and protest marchers into the teeth of segregation in the South. Her second request was wiser: she asked me to be sure to talk with the elders before getting my ticket and going.

The three elders at the time, Dewey Carlson, Nicholas Schank, and Dr. George Hallenbeck, were all seasoned parishioners of Grace whose support and good judgment were of great value to me. They all were at least thirty years my senior, and while well versed in the best of Lutheran ways and deeply loyal to the Lutheran tradition, they — like most other Lutherans — had little experience in social protest in areas as volatile as race. Grace Church had no African-American members; River Forest had no black residents. I called them together and made my case for attending the March on Washington: I would pay my own way, go on my day off, and behave myself nonviolently. Their response, while measured, was all I could ask for and made me proud to be their pastor: "Do what in your conscience as a pastor you believe God directs you to do, and remember that not all the people of Grace will feel as you do about Dr. King and the March on Washington."

I left the parsonage early on the morning of August 28, clerical collar securely around my neck and Beverly's blessing upon my head, to join a chartered planeload of people heading for the March on Washington. En route I struck up conversations with a few of those whom I knew, but for the most part it was quiet on board, as everyone felt some apprehension about just what to expect. In Washington we were bussed to locations near the Capitol mall, as near as a crowd of some 200,000 allowed. I was ashamed of any misgivings I had harbored about the March. In fact, there were tears in my eyes as I stood at curbside watching wave after wave of delegations of black Americans from Southern cities and towns marching by, their faces beaming with smiles, the men dressed in their Sunday best with shirts starched and suits well pressed, the women neatly dressed and most wearing their Sunday hats, their shoes spotlessly whitened. Many were well along in years, and I could not help but wonder how many were the grandchildren, if not the children, of slaves who could only pray, sing, and dream of such a day as this. I followed along to a place somewhere on the sidelines of the Mall Reflecting Pool and listened to the songs of Bob Dylan and Peter, Paul and Mary, followed by warm-up speeches by Roy Wilkins of the NAACP and Jackie Robinson of the Brooklyn Dodgers.

But the March on Washington changed from an outing to a crusade when Martin Luther King, Jr., took his turn at the podium. Few of us were prepared for the stunning, lasting impact of his "I Have a Dream" speech. Never before nor since have I heard a person "sustain the weary with a word," as Isaiah wrote, or make the prophetic vision more compelling to loose the bonds of wickedness, undo the thongs of the yoke, and let the oppressed go free. I felt goose bumps riding up and down my spine as King came to that majestic concluding peroration: "Free at last, free at last . . . thank God almighty, we are free at last!" King held before us the vision of a day when the sons of slaves and the sons of slaveholders could sit together at the table of brotherhood.

I marched with the children of slaveholders that day. The hard work was for the heirs of slaveholders to take their place at the table of brotherhood. That was on my mind as I returned home that evening. I knew history was being made on August 28 and that, if my children or grandchildren would one day ask me whether I was there, I was grateful to be able to say Yes. On returning to Grace, I remembered the counsel of the elders about the importance of how I interpreted my participation to those who saw it differently. In my sermon the following Sunday, I mentioned Martin Luther King's speech and my experience of the day in Washington as one that was as orderly and impressive as a giant Sunday school picnic. I said little more about it publicly and asked for those who questioned my participation to give me the chance to speak with them personally — which, of course, no one did. In all likelihood, some of the parishioners, less than ecstatic about my going to the March, held their peace in the hope that this, too, would pass, and that the young new senior pastor, six months along in office, would leave racial waters nearer home undisturbed. I knew I had to proceed with care and wisdom in dispelling that illusion; and I was determined to keep any prophetic pastoral leadership I was capable of offering inseparable from clear-cut biblical underpinning.

My first opportunity to do so came in an unexpected development connected with a memorial to my predecessor. Remembering Otto Geiseman's forty years of pastoral ministry at Grace was on my mind during his final days and in the weeks following his death. A variety of opinions came out, many of which had to do with adding to the furnishings in the sanctuary. One of them was to complete the original plan for the chancel area, which called for a hand-carved wooden canopy over the baptismal font to match the exquisite altar reredos and chancel adornments crafted years before in Italy. The placement of the font under the south transept of the nave, however, made the idea unworkable, as I recalled Otto himself saying.

My thought was to remember his ministry by establishing a mission program that would initiate new ministries needed for this new time. His whole theology was centered on the Kingdom of God, and his practice favored crossing frontiers of pastoral counseling and involvement in the community; neither of those areas was overcrowded with Lutheran clergy at the time. Kingdom Frontiers, then, became the name given to a memorial fund to seed new mission ventures that were not yet recognized by the church or that needed a onetime grant to fill out a program not fully funded. In proposing to name the fund Kingdom Frontiers instead of the O. A. Geiseman Memorial, I was following a principle he had established early on that no name plaques of donors of prominent gifts be placed in the sanctuary or anywhere throughout the building. He did not disparage major gifts, but he did not want them singled out by name at the expense of all the others who had given sacrificially but in lesser proportion. Following that practice led to one of my first minor scrapes. Two women whom I knew well and respected highly, Clara Amling and Virginia Beardsley, spoke to me on behalf of others who saw my suggestion for the naming of the fund as an unworthy slight to the memory of the man for whom it was established. That the principle of not naming a memorial originated with Geiseman himself did not mollify them, however, and after some discussion we arrived at an acceptable compromise: Kingdom Frontiers, The O. A. Geiseman Memorial Fund. It was an early lesson for me on how easy it is for good intentions to be misunderstood and on the importance of listening rather than bristling.

The first Kingdom Frontiers mission project connected Grace to one of Chicago's toughest black ghetto areas, the Robert Taylor Homes housing project, which crammed some 28,000 people in high-rise apartments along the Dan Ryan Expressway on Chicago's south side. Seven young pre-seminarians from Concordia Senior College in Fort Wayne, Indiana — Grace parishioners Joel Zeddies and Jeff Thorsen among them — spent the summer of 1964 ringing doorbells, coaching kids, teaching Sunday school, and getting a glimpse of what life is like in an inner-city area with a high crime rate. They worked under Pastor Albert Pero, an African-American mission pastor who had earlier begun a Lutheran mission congregation in an area storefront chapel. That eleven-week beginning was continued throughout the following year by Kingdom Frontiers' sponsorship of two seminarian vicars, David Drechsler and Les Kimball. Serving in that area meant contact with gangs, and one of the more unusual results of the connection between Grace Church and the Robert Taylor Homes through Kingdom Frontiers was the several evenings of meetings between Black Panther gangbangers and the Grace elders in the church's reception room. The sessions were intended to begin even the most cursory link between people of two vastly different worlds — which existed scarcely ten miles apart. Grace members had put $6000 into this opening venture of Kingdom Frontiers and authorized another $4000 for its continuance. Five more young adults from Grace — Ron Baasch, Jack Kolzow, James Mack, Mary Zeddies, and Janet Zumack — volunteered as Sunday school teachers in a mission congregation of 161 baptized and 54 communicant members, which was soon formed as Holy Trinity Lutheran Church. Tentative as it all seemed, and wildly improbable that young, white, suburban Lutherans could make any difference in the Robert Taylor Homes, it made me glad that something local and real was bringing black and white, ghetto and suburban people together. It was a venture for educating Grace's membership no less than serving Holy Trinity. Here was at least one way we could bring the towering rhetoric of Martin Luther King's "Dream" speech down to earth in our small corner of the vineyard. The Kingdom Frontiers program would continue into future years and expand into scores of mission support projects at home and abroad — as it continues to this day.

Another pastoral effort in bridge-building across turbulent racial waters during the mid-1960s began because of my close friendship with Pastor Don Becker of the historic First Immanuel Lutheran Church on Ashland Boulevard and Roosevelt Road on Chicago's west side. He and I had vicared together in Japan ten years earlier, and our continuing friendship here was instrumental in forming interracial Bible study groups that alternated monthly meetings in the homes of Grace and First Immanuel parishioners. Before announcing plans for the program to our congregation, I asked Don to join me in conversation with our Board of Elders, and I went with him to meet the First Immanuel leaders, including Jamesia Manning and Willa Chase, two remarkable black women who formed long-lasting friendships with our members Flora Sandvoss, Clark and Marion Miller, James and Margo Ladwig, Paul and Irma Merriweather, and others who recognized the importance of biblical study that spanned the abyss of increasingly ugly racial riots. In time, the interracial Bible study groups would include First St. Paul's, St. Stephen's, and Ebenezer Lutheran churches of Chicago and Grace Church, Northbook, as partners with Grace in helping people to know each other personally across racial boundaries during a decade when relations between black and white populations were as burdened as ever by the blight of so many decades of racial injustice. Little publicity was sought or given to these modest efforts; it was timidity more than lack of public relations know-how that kept these quiet but steady efforts virtually unknown.

I was skittish about the reaction Grace members would have when they read news stories or saw pictures of black Lutherans walking into the homes and apartments of other Grace members. I am ashamed of myself when I think back on it. Major press stories in September 1966 covered the cursing of Martin Luther King and the rock-throwing that seriously hurt twelve of his protestors in the Cicero march; National Guardsmen were called in with their bayonets drawn to prevent wholesale mayhem against the protestors. Those were the matters that dominated the headlines. We would have done well to have been far more bold in telling our less spectacular stories of less visible contact but more lasting, personal understanding forged between people simply trying to read the Bible together with connections to the times.

The Women's Society of Grace added another link to the connection between First Immanuel and Grace by sponsoring an Adopt-A-Child program for the nursery school that began in 1963 at First Immanuel — another outgrowth of my friendship and partnership with Don Becker. Our women made this program a regular part of their budget and have continued support for it nearly forty years into the present, with occasional visits between women of both congregations to see the fruits of their common labors.

In the late 1970s, Grace and First Immanuel were among the dozen or more Lutheran congregations that formed Lutheran Congregations for Career Development (LCCD). This was a network that brought together men and women in corporate departments of human resources with inner-city high-school youth of Lutheran parishes, to meet face to face; it was an effort to help disadvantaged kids see reasons for staying in school, and to broaden their horizons of the possibilities for finding good work. Harold Hurrelbrink, an executive in an office furniture firm, and Alice Pursell, who worked at Marshall Field's downtown store, were among the Grace members who took part in this program.

The congregation also had a literal taste of the LCCD at work during summer Sundays, when loaves of bread baked by minority youths were offered for sale after Sunday services. When graduates of the LCCD program came to Grace for Sunday morning presentations, and some spoke as lawyers, seminarians, and accountants as well as plumbers, truck drivers, and salespeople, they were living reminders to the congregants of the importance of getting out of our own suburban, upper-middle-class ghettos and forging partnerships with congregations of the city.

Kingdom Frontiers was introduced to the congregation in an illustrated brochure that commercial artist Jim Ladwig of the congregation had designed, including the striking logo that gave the program the visual symbol it needed. The success of that public-relations piece prompted me to begin communicating regularly with the parish about all aspects of congregational life and mission, something that had never happened at Grace before, other than on anniversaries or major fund-raising occasions. We needed a parish communication: *Grace Notes* was the answer. It began in the summer of 1964 with a front-page story, with pictures, of the renovated sanctuary of Grace Church, which was re-dedicated on September 20 of that year (at a cost of $22,953).

The interior of the church had never been painted. Pastor Geiseman had held out for leaving the walls and ceiling natural in the manner of European cathedrals. But the walls of those cathedrals were of stone; Grace Church's walls were primarily of plaster and by the 1960s looked much the worse for a third of a century of wear. The trustees, Bruce Goodman, Ray Amling, and Carl Sievert, drew in Ernest Fedler and Milton Tatter for help on the Renovation Committee. Carl Eilers advised us on rewiring the ever-problematic sound system; Perry Hugh constructed new cabinetry for the system; Wayne Schroeder provided needed counsel on the right shade and type of paint; and head janitor Guenther Gutgesell, who painted the entire interior by himself twenty years later, made sure the clouds of dust, fallen plaster, and dirt were cleaned up Sunday by Sunday. Thus all the misgivings about the renovation were put to rest. The restored interior set off the stunning beauty of the stained-glass windows, and in the course of our restoring the chan-

cel carvings I was fascinated by an old photograph of the Italian crafts-
man and his four sons carving the reredos, pulpit, lectern, and chancel
appointments in the 1930s. Acoustics in the sanctuary became clearer
and more resonant with this renovation, which was important because
Grace Church was and is a location frequently chosen for organ and
choral recording by groups from near and far.

Issues of *Grace Notes* carried stories and pictures on everything we
were doing. I wrote the contents of each issue, and since it appeared
quarterly throughout the 1960s, it gave me a new opportunity to reach
the membership regularly in the written word as well as from the pulpit. During the 1970s I moved to pastoral letters as a more adequate
medium for reaching the parish twelve times a year, with greater con-
centration on fewer things I considered of primary importance. But
Grace Notes was invaluable to me as I began to place my pastoral stamp
on Grace Church in a time of transition within the congregation and
turbulence in the world outside the parish walls. In putting the issues
together, I was helped by many parishioners skilled in the print media
and photography. The end product was appealing as an illustrated parish news piece that strengthened the ties of belonging within the congregation through a decade when too many congregations were falling
apart.

The historic Second Vatican Council, called by Pope John XXIII, began
to make its influence felt locally. I had come to know Father John Fahey
of nearby St. Luke's Catholic parish as a friend who was as open as I was
to inter-parish contact. During the Week of Christian Unity in January
1968, we collaborated in an ecumenical service at St. Luke's in which he
led prayers and I preached. I was glad to see Grace Church well represented, especially by parishioners whose spouses were Roman Catholic
and who had waited long for this day. Hazel Hanley was present with
her husband, and Alfred Korbel sat with his wife in worship; each of
them had been trained from childhood never to even enter a Catholic or
Lutheran church building, let alone sit together to hear Scripture and
pray. It also pleased me that Grace was well represented in the Living
Room Dialogs that followed in later months, which met alternately in

the homes of Grace and St. Luke parishioners. Ralph Gehrke, Rudolf and Mildred Heinze, and Wayne and Phyllis Lucht were among the Grace members on the Concordia Teachers College faculty who brought substance to these meetings.

Richard Beeman, John O'Neil of St. Luke's, and Sister Jean Murray of the Rosary College faculty were among the Catholics whom our members and I came to know as we laid the groundwork for later, broader cooperation. Sister Jean went on to become president of Rosary College (now renamed Dominican University), and Marion Miller, one of our Dialog participants and my secretary for ten years, became her administrative assistant there. Other Grace members, Hildegarde Schmidt and Meg Busse, to name two, also joined the Dominican University staff in positions of major responsibility in the admissions office. Grace members also benefited as students at Dominican, including our daughter Ann, who was well taught in the Gospel of John by Sister Mary Mulherne as she completed her college education there. During that year the Dominican chancellor, Sister Candida Lund, called me in a mild panic because they needed our Fellowship Hall for a major musical recital that had lost its place at Dominican due to a booking error. When I called Sister Candida not long after that — in what might well be called a bit of ecumenical backscratching — she opened up the Gothic beauty of the University's dining hall as a reception dinner location for Ann's wedding.

St. Luke's parishioners John O'Neil and Richard Beeman have been friends and collaborators in community labors through the years; whenever I see them, I am uplifted by the memory of who they are as fellow Christians since those early days of Living Room Dialogs. Another outcome of those early ecumenical contacts was the introduction of the joint Services of Scripture and Prayer in the parochial schools of Grace and St. Luke. When children saw and experienced their respective pastors together in worship and preaching, it gave their young minds a glimpse of the length and breadth and height of Christ's love at work in bringing together members of his Body who had too long been separated. Also, the removal in those years of the offensive Catholic prenuptial requirement that the children of mixed couples be baptized and raised as Catholics was a welcome application of Vatican II ecumenism where it counted most — in the lives, marriages, and families of Christians of both traditions. I began to receive invitations to participate in joint wedding services when one of our young men married a Catholic bride, and welcomed priests to join me when the bride was from Grace Church. On Reformation weekend in late October 1968, I participated in a Catholic-Lutheran conference in Albuquerque, New Mexico, and preached for the Sunday morning joint worship. What I recall from that occasion was the wry comment of the priest, who leaned over to me and whispered his relief that he did not have to sing "A Mighty Fortress Is *Your* God."

My participation in local Protestant ecumenical ties began in the mid-1960s as well. I joined the Ministerial Association and attended the monthly meetings that enabled me to meet clergy and gain a closer sense of how River Forest and Oak Park congregations approached ministry to the community, especially on the hot issue of those times — racial integration. Oak Park was well ahead of River Forest in confronting redlining and other forms of racial injustice common to Chicago suburbs. My witness as a River Forest pastor involved in interracial Bible study groups at Grace was a modest sign of one place in which to begin pastoral leadership in a community with deeply embedded — albeit more subtly hidden — racial prejudices. The boldness and courage of Charles Jarvis of First Methodist and Ray Johnson of First Baptist in Oak Park impressed me as they spoke prophetically to the community through the local press and participated in demonstrations against racial injustice. I was less experienced than they were in public ministry, but I found it valuable to listen and learn in Ministerial Association meetings.

A later opportunity for local ecumenism, and more effective by far, came when I joined a dozen other clergy — mostly Protestant but with a few Catholic priests included — for weekly study of the Common Lectionary texts that all of us were following. Each Friday morning we began with breakfast and prayer, followed by a study of the three biblical texts appointed for the Sunday ten days hence, thus giving us a running start on sermon preparation. Though other agenda were suggested from time to time, the group stayed with the singular purpose of lectionary study related to preaching, which was the reason why it has lasted for over twenty years and became for me the most significant pastoral support network of my ministry. Doctrinal differences were present, of course, but they were penultimate under the power of the Word. It was not the time or place to make points on each other, which would have killed the whole idea in short order. It was a time to listen to the Word together, to offer the best each had to offer, to receive new insight from one another in connecting text and congregation, and to *enjoy* one another's friendship.

As we grew in mutual trust and respect for each other, we found occasions to be pastors to each other. David Robertson of River Forest Presbyterian and Greg Dell of Euclid Methodist heard my confession and spoke Christ's absolution to me in times when I needed a pastor. I will never forget the morning that Austin Boulevard Christian Church pastor Don McCord came a few minutes late, brushed aside any mention of breakfast, and all but sank to his knees beside us at the table to tell us about his son: as a young doctor serving Indians and Eskimos on the northernmost shore of Alaska, the younger McCord had gone through the ice off the Arctic Ocean shore when he was blinded by a once-in-a-century blizzard while driving his snow tractor vehicle to a remote village. We put everything aside immediately and gathered Don McCord in our arms, prayed for his son, wept with him, and began a vigil of whatever help we could offer him and his congregation as he and Ann made the long journey in search of their son's body, which was never found. Moments like that were ecumenism at the deepest level: holding onto each other in grief and hope in the face of the sudden, brutal shock of death. When I told Grace parishioners what such ecumenism meant in my ministry in and beyond the parish, I never heard a word of objection, and I did get many words of appreciation. It was more than surface approval: Grace parishioners expected meaningful leadership in local ecumenism as a response in deed to what they expressed in word every Sunday in the Nicene Creed: "We believe in one holy catholic and apostolic Church." I have never understood why more clergy in our community did not show interest in a lectionary study when invited to take part and why I have so rarely found any form of it wherever I have traveled with inquiries about clergy ecumenism at the grassroots level.

The late 1960s also brought opportunities to expand my ministry through membership on several boards, always with the knowledge and approval of the Grace board of elders. Serving on the Commission on Historical Publications with John Tietjen, Eric Heintzen, and Wilbur Rosin gave me one of the most enjoyable and purposeful experiences I have had while a member of the ministerium of the Missouri Synod. I looked forward to Heintzen's steady leadership in meetings that were often held in our reception room at Grace Church. Joining the board of the Christian Century Foundation, publisher of the *Christian Century* magazine, began an association — now in its fourth decade — with editors Kyle Haselden, Alan Geyer, James Wall, and now John Buchanan, plus lay board leaders of the caliber of Robert Crowe, James McClure, Lydia Talbot, and Richard McAuliffe. They widened my pastoral horizon continually, and they enabled me to contribute what pastoral ministry at Grace gave me to offer in furthering the mission of this key journal devoted to interpreting the intersection of faith and life in the American church and society.

A similar opportunity to help guide the direction of a magazine and see to its support came when I joined the editorial board of *The American Lutheran*, an independent journal speaking from our denomination to issues of Lutheran unity and mission here and abroad. We met annually in New York City, where budget limits meant we slept not at the Waldorf Astoria but at the Seaman's Mission in Lower Manhattan. With colleagues Arthur Carl Piepkorn, Richard Koenig, Ted Whitrock, and Alfred Meyer participating, the meetings with editor Glenn Stone were stimulating for my pastoral work as well as productive for the magazine. I admired Piepkorn as one of my premier teachers at Concordia Seminary and greatly respected his combined gifts of meticulous scholarship and humane high churchmanship. As his roommate at the Seaman's Mission, I also came to know another aspect of this splendid man, whom I had never seen before without black suit and clerical collar: he could fall asleep quickly and he snored loudly.

Speaking invitations began to come my way during those years, and the experience of preparing to address clergy and lay groups always meant drawing directly from my pastoral work at Grace as grist for the mill of my speech. At a conference on race sponsored by the Lutheran Human Relations Association at Valparaiso University, I met the patriarch among Lutheran pioneers in racial reconciliation, Andrew Schulze, whose rumpled suit, sad eyes, and understated manner were surface appearances covering a heart and mind that were relentless in summoning Lutherans to recognize what we had to learn and to give in the exhausting work of battling entrenched racial bias in the church and the nation. I also shared the speaker podium with the young Stanley Hauerwas, who spoke about the sin of racism with a fearless prophetic voice and a salty vocabulary that startled Lutherans unused to talk that blunt from the lecture podium. My mother came to Valparaiso for that conference, and seeing her in the front row heartened me to bear witness to the spirit of racial understanding I had received from her throughout my childhood and beyond, and to say that all was not lost in suburbia, at least not in the small corner of it that I served.

At the invitation of the Southeastern District of the Missouri Synod, I traveled to Roanoke, Virginia, to speak on the role of the pastoral ministry in the formation of ethics in an America increasingly in need of an ethically sound laity. That conference was my first opportunity to meet Dr. Jacob A. O. Preus, then the president of Concordia Seminary in Springfield, Illinois, and soon to be elected by ultraconservatives to the synodical presidency in an election riven by shameful electioneering that eventually put him and Grace Church on a collision course. His cordiality to me was amiable but without depth, an impression that would be confirmed before several years had passed, when he and I came head to head in a church struggle that eventually led to Grace Church's withdrawal from the Missouri Synod and a legal battle over the Grace property that required the Supreme Court to finally settle.

In those busy years of establishing my identity in the Grace pastorate, I was approached to stand as a candidate for the presidency of the English District of the Missouri Synod, a nongeographical district that was noted for its progressive stance on mission and wider Lutheran ties. Because I was fully committed to parish-based ministry, and increasingly mindful of how much it meant to serve at Grace Church, I declined, and I never regretted that decision. Speaking to collegians at Purdue University in an early September 1966 conference of Gamma Delta, a national network of the Lutheran collegiate ministry, was lively despite the misery of hay fever that had given me late-summer woes from my teen years onward. Since I spoke through a runny nose most of the day, I was treated to a banquet roast in the evening that featured a spoof of me, face covered with a tablecloth-sized handkerchief that filtered out most of the rehash of what I had said, except for the Hugh Hefner references (*Playboy* magazine having recently emerged as the slick bearer of the sexual revolution of the 1960s). I was learning what communicated and what did not, and what I gained from these speaking excursions always came back to the parish from the pulpit or in my pastoral letters.

When I received an invitation from Granger Westberg, then the dean of Lutheran advocates for bridging the gap between theology and medicine, to attend an exploratory meeting on continuing pastoral education, I accepted it, hardly knowing that it would bear so directly on my pastoral future. I had come to respect any idea in Granger Westberg's head as I got to know him during his days on the faculties of the University of Chicago Divinity School and Medical School (in this he was unique in America, but it was only one of his unique ventures). He secured a $5,000 grant from the Lilly Foundation to gather a dozen of us from various denominations in Houston on Easter Monday, 1968. All of us were parish pastors, and we arrived bushed from Lent and Holy Week schedules. But that made no difference to Westberg, who plunged immediately into the subject of continuing education for clergy modeled after the American Association of General Practitioners in the medical field. He saw parish pastors as generalists who were also specialists, much as GP doctors were generalists of their own special genre in the wider field of medicine. In a tightly packed Monday and Tuesday, with no time off except to eat, we heard him out on his vision of a national organization of clergy that would focus on ministry as a lifetime of growth in the art and skills of our vocation, with practicing clergy themselves as the teachers who would share the practice of their parish ministries. The response of ideas and creative suggestions came so thick and fast that by the supper hour on Tuesday we were drooping, and Granger knew it. His timely surprise was to introduce to us a Baptist Buick dealer, who hosted us for a steak dinner and baseball game at the Astrodome. Appropriately, the game turned out to be the longest night game in the history of baseball: the Houston Astros and New York Mets played twenty-three innings before the Astro second basemen, somewhere around 2 a.m., providentially erred on a ground ball, which allowed the Mets to win — which allowed us all to go back to the hotel and sleep. We had to sleep fast, though, because on Wednesday morning came Granger Westberg's wrap-up, during which the groundwork was laid for the Academy of Parish Clergy. That organization continues to this day as a national network for congregation-based clergy who help each other grow through sharing the practice. I am a grateful beneficiary of its functions and of the lifelong friendships I have thus made with clergy throughout the nation.

*   *   *

Throughout the middle and late 1960s, the problem of our nation's involvement in the civil war in Vietnam grew in tragic seriousness year by year. The euphemism of United States armed forces as "advisors" was dropped in January 1965, and young Americans were sent by the thousands as soldiers, sailors, and marines to fight the Communist forces of North Vietnam in a war that was never legally declared by Congress. Americans were instantly and deeply divided over the war, which soon ranked with race, the sexual revolution, the nuclear threat, the Communist menace, and the Free Speech Movement as one more fissure in the fabric of American society. We felt it at Grace Church. As our young members and their families struggled with the moral issues involved, they needed pastoral guidance. I sent a letter to ones I knew were facing the draft, inviting them to come to the church for a series of informal discussions in which I sought to inform their consciences rather than dictate what conscience told them to do. My role was that of a moderator, listener, and intercessor as conversations proceeded in earnest among those who had the most at stake. I invited older members who had faced similar dilemmas during the Korean conflict to tell their stories. Those stories differed strikingly: Eugene Lewis spoke as a conscientious objector who rendered nonmilitary service to the country; Jim Sutton was a jet fighter pilot who flew missions over North Korea. One of our young men chose the new alternative that emerged during the Vietnam War, that of going to Canada to avoid the draft; several others chose conscientious-objector status. Others volunteered or were drafted. But the majority of Grace's young men who were of age to go to war never did because of their status as college or graduate school students. I don't recall that any individual was judged for the choice he made; the subject was too complicated at the time for any of us to presume full clarity of moral vision.

However, on Sunday, March 17, 1968, the gospel for the day was from Luke 9:54ff., the story of Jesus' rebuke of the disciples who had asked him to call down fire from heaven to consume the Samaritans who rejected his determination to go the way of the cross. I felt compelled by the text to break my silence from the pulpit on the agony of Vietnam. The sermon, entitled "What Manner of Spirit Are You?" contained these excerpts:

> This gnawing, cancerous spirit of accepting the destruction of others as a way of solving human problems is now before us because the text makes it unavoidable. . . . During the past week the number of American men killed in Vietnam passed 20,000. God alone knows the numbers of Vietnamese who have been killed and maimed by the 100,000 tons of napalm dropped on them by our bombers, yet not a single square foot in Vietnam has been secured. . . . In the name of my Lord Jesus Christ, I say that this mayhem must stop. I also speak on behalf of the American Marine who wrote home one day before he was killed in Vietnam: "This war has gone to hell . . . little brother, you do anything not to come over here. It's hell. It's not like the war Dad fought in . . . you don't know who or why you're fighting. . . ." I ask you now to do three things as your conscience guides you. The first is to

write a personal letter to your congressman, with a firm No to the continuance of our nation's policy in Vietnam. Second, we must sacrifice in behalf of the refugees who are ravaged by war, and there is a way to do that. Reach deep into your pocket to give generously to Lutheran World Relief and Church World Service. While the world chatters about saving face, the people of Christ are called to bind up the wounded and help the distraught. The third is to pray for the guidance of Almighty God, to whom all of us belong whatever our race or nationality, for our own leaders, our servicemen, our enemies, and especially the civilian men, women, and children who suffer the most, and for all peacemakers who labor for justice and righteousness to prevail. . . .

There was no neutral response to that sermon. As I greeted Grace members from my usual place in the narthex after the benediction, the lines were long either to support or oppose my application of the Luke 9 text. To all who waited patiently to favor or object to the sermon, I could only beg them to make the Word their guide. I was not surprised by the intensity of the response, for I had felt it while I was preaching. Nor did I take offense at the woman who had torn up her check intended for the offering and placed the bits of paper in my hand instead. Nor could I fail to be moved by the parents whose son was in Vietnam and whose strong handshake was firm in support of the Word proclaimed. That sermon, that Sunday, was a defining moment in the continuing, complex process of becoming the pastor of Grace: I had preached a difficult text with conviction that it fit an even more difficult situation.

Less than a month after that sermon, Martin Luther King, Jr., was shot dead in Memphis, followed immediately by the eruption of even more violent riots in Chicago, Baltimore, Washington, and Cincinnati. Lyndon Johnson told the nation he would not run for president in the fall election. Students at Columbia University trashed the administrative offices after shutting down classes in protest of the war. In early June, Robert Kennedy was assassinated in a Los Angeles hotel kitchen. In August, chaos ruled inside the Democratic National Convention, while outside in Grant Park the Chicago police conducted what was called a "police riot" against war protestors. As before in the '60s, these were not tranquil times.

Yet, despite the social upheavals of the late 1960s, ministry in the congregation went on. The preaching and teaching of the gospel and the administering of the sacraments held us together, giving us glimpses of how the Word creates its own alternate world where the community of faith can not only survive but thrive. In numbers, the Grace membership reached just over 2,000 baptized, with the communicant membership at 1,652. In September 1968, Dr. Ralph Gehrke began a series of Sunday morning Bible classes on the Apocrypha, a suitable subject for the times. During the same month, the Grace Young Adults heard Robert Short, author of *The Gospel According to Peanuts,* present an illustrated program on the famed cartoon character. The high schoolers resumed their schedule of two Sunday evening meetings each month, with twenty-one parishioners serving as counselors and sponsors for the Freshman-Sophomore and the Junior-Senior groups. Frances Wetzel led off the September meeting of the Women's Society with a picture report on her recent journey to Nigeria, and the Men's Club heard Joseph Kitagawa of the University of Chicago Divinity School speak on the global mission of the gospel in a turbulent world.

Along with and under these congregational events, the gracious mystery of the Holy Spirit's working went on in myriad ways, most of them outside my awareness. Some were surprises of grace, as when Arthur Wellman came to tell me how a hymn sung during a Sunday service had released him from the burden of years of a marriage that had died when his wife turned against him, their newborn son, and life in general as a result of postpartum psychosis. He quoted this verse from Georg Neumark's sturdy chorale "If Thou But Suffer God to Guide Thee":

> God knows full well when times of gladness
> Shall be the needful thing for thee,
> When he has tried thy soul with sadness
> And from all guile has found thee free,
> He comes to thee all unaware
> And makes thee own his loving care.

Arthur then spoke of the fine woman he had met, one who had known her share of sorrow in losing her spouse, and of their plans for marriage, which had filled the emptiness of his personal life with happiness. It was a sign of my becoming his pastor, not his chaplain, that he could reveal the marvel of the grace that had come upon him and the unexpected way it reached him. Becoming a pastor rather than a chaplain to another family took place under vastly different circumstances. Their teenage granddaughter had gone berserk while baby-sitting, and had stabbed the infant to death with an ice pick. Thus began a yearlong saga of pastoral care for a young woman stumbling her way through the labyrinth of the jails and mental hospitals of Illinois. First it was the Cook County Jail; then came years of dreary confinement in the old county mental hospital at Dunning; then it was a lot of drifting, "wandering in desert wastes, finding no way to a city to dwell in, hungry and thirsty, soul fainting within," as Psalm 107:4-5 describes it. Finally she returned to Chicago to bear her own daughter, who died only a few days after her birth. On a bitter-cold winter day, this mother, now old before her time but whose once-radiant face as a child I still remembered from her first communion, stood with the undertaker and me, the three of us shivering as the tiny body of her infant daughter was committed to the earth and to her Father in heaven. The father on earth's whereabouts were unknown.

Becoming a pastor meant welcoming home Bill Hartmann from his Rhodes Scholarship at Oxford, and coaching him in keeping his faith as his spiritual compass while he taught at Michigan State University in the rarified world of sound-wave physics. Becoming a pastor to Clara Kipple meant working with her to form a Lutheran Singles Group for widows and widowers in the middle and later years. This fellowship and service group soon drew widely from Grace and other congregations and also became a meeting place for singles who were later married, including Clara herself. She married Carl Sievert, and they both enjoyed being teased as the couple who achieved what many others hoped to achieve. Becoming a pastor meant giving names and pastoral support to Hank Hasselbring, a successful insurance man who made time for and set a priority on excellence in our Sunday school during his ten years as superintendent.

Becoming a pastor in the 1960s and early '70s happened as the art of my ministry developed as I honed the skills of preaching, teaching, liturgy, counseling, staff administration, stewardship, and mission outreach. As tumultuous change engulfed American life, which the congregation and I certainly felt at Grace Church, there was grace sufficient to keep us on course. Though preaching was often disparaged during that time of activism, and the pastoral role was seen by some more as an agent for social change than as a caregiver for souls, I do not recall awakening on any morning without a sense of being called to offer the good news that Jesus is Lord for every bad situation. This was not permission to gloat; it was incentive to serve that gospel, with fidelity to the faith handed down to me in the great tradition of the church catholic, and to apply it creatively in circumstances that were new and daunting almost daily.

Becoming the pastor did not depend on having all the answers, to be sure, but in doing the next thing in the face of whatever came along. My ministry was expressed through new ventures with the congregation in response to outside pressures and calamities: the Kingdom Frontiers mission into tough neighborhoods; the interracial Bible study groups as race riots literally lit up Chicago's west side; the ecumenical contacts; the board memberships; Vietnam decision sessions; Lutheran Congregations for Career Development; the Academy of Parish Clergy; and speaking opportunities beyond the congregation. Yet I spent the bulk of the days of these years of my pastorate carrying out ministry within the congregation, what I call "everydayishness." For me that meant taking what came day by day, attending to routines of morning study, afternoon visitation of the sick and aged, and evenings with counseling and the inevitable meetings (which, like the poor, we have always with us). It indeed meant savoring time with Beverly and our young children, with whom I could walk to my work and their school on most days, singing songs and playing games with Ann, Chris, Sarah, and Joel as they made their way through Grace School. Everydayishness was not boredom or hand-over-hand sameness; it was receiving the overwhelming goodness of people and their love as sustenance for my daily work. A symbol for all of that was a frequent morning ritual of Brad Froehlig, a primary grade youngster of Grace School, who would knock on my study door and ask, "Well, Pastor, how are things going?" How *were* things going? By the grace of the Lord, very much as the Psalmist David described everydayishness in the closing verse of Psalm 121: "The Lord will keep your coming in and your going out from this time on and forevermore."

Yet, as the 1970s set in, just over the horizon another storm was gathering that would shake the congregation and test my pastoral leadership as nothing before.

CHAPTER 5

Ministry Tested

We do not bear in mind enough that no Christian commu-
nity comes together without a seed of discord.

DIETRICH BONHOEFFER

On July 20, 1969, the day that astronaut Neil Armstrong announced his
"one small step" onto the moon as "one giant leap for mankind," I was
stepping into the ancient Roman amphitheater in Caesarea, about to
conclude a month-long study tour of Israel, and reading a letter from my
assistant pastor, Philip Bruening. The letter told of another event occur-
ring several thousands of miles to the west, one that would hardly rank
on a par with the moon landing, but would in its own way hold giant-
leap implications for our congregation and denomination. The Missouri Synod, gathered in convention in Denver, Colorado, had taken
two steps that could not have been more contradictory. First, the ultraconservatives had succeeded in electing their man, Jacob A. O. Preus, to
the presidency of the Synod, ousting incumbent Oliver Harms. Then
the moderate conservatives (simple "conservative" and "liberal" are
largely useless terms in this discussion) swung enough votes to approve
pulpit and altar fellowship with the American Lutheran Church.

This improbable combination broke open a long-standing denominational tension between two strands within the Synod: one was marked by a narrow reading of Lutheran theology, which at its worst resulted in doctrinal sterility, legalism in clergy practice, and strict isolation from the rest of Christendom; the other strand stood for an evangelical tradition that took doctrine no less seriously but centered it in the gospel as the power for faith active in love in pastoral practice and an openness to other Christians. The two strands had managed to exist side by side since the Synod's founding in 1847 — without hardening into opposing parties so fractious as to split the church body. Synodical conventions, prior to 1969, had been notable for an unofficial tradition, respected by most clergy and lay delegates, that made political campaigning the kiss of death for anyone seeking office, particularly the presidential office. That tradition was respected by most — but not all.

For years ultraconservatives had published scathing newsletters attacking their targeted opponents, including Otto Geiseman, and promoting their favorites. Finally, in 1945, a group of forty-four synodical churchmen, Geiseman among them with Grace Church support, published a booklet entitled "A Statement," which protested the growing theological stagnation and legalism they saw as choking the free course of the gospel. When the then Synod president, John Behnken, appealed for the withdrawal of "A Statement," the signers complied, and the Synod lived on for another quarter of a century in denial of the needed theological work. Theological change was happening, and the ultraconservative gripe was legitimate. But their tactics were not. They brought Jacob Preus to Missouri Synod leadership via unprecedented slander and shameless electioneering by a highly efficient cohort that labored while many of us slept. It would take some time after the 1969 Denver convention before most LCMS clergy, including me, would gradually awaken to the long-term consequences of Preus's election. He and his cohort were bent on eliminating all who did not march lockstep with their determination to turn the Missouri Synod into a monolith of Lutheran fundamentalism — purged of evangelical moderates and isolated from the rest of Christendom. This is the background essential for understanding the storm that shook the Synod, its faculties, mission leaders, and congregations throughout the 1970s. And it shook Grace Lutheran Church with an intensity born of our unique circumstances.

Walter Christopher, our delegate to the Denver convention, reported on the convention to Grace members on a warm August evening soon after he returned. Chicago papers had covered the general story in detail, but our members needed to hear the fascinating story under the story. How could the staid, unflappable clergy and laity of the Missouri Synod turn in such a Janus-headed performance in voting Harms out and Preus in and then offer the hand of fellowship to another, more liberal branch of Lutherans? And who was this Jacob Preus? Answers to both questions were sketchy at best. Christopher did portray the new president as a traveler between Lutheran Synods around whom controversy had always gathered.

Son of the governor of Minnesota, Dr. Preus, together with his brother, Robert, had lodged accusations against the doctrinal soundness of faculty and administrative leaders in his former church body, the Evangelical Lutheran Church. He then moved on to his next synod, the tiny, ultraconservative Norwegian-oriented Evangelical Lutheran Synod, where in 1955 he and his brother led the movement to break fellowship with the Missouri Synod. Then, abruptly and with no explanation, he joined the Missouri Synod in 1958 as a faculty member of Concordia Seminary in Springfield, Illinois, where he became president in 1962. Ultraconservatives in the LCMS astutely sized him up as their man to promote for the Synod presidency, a choice he did not discourage, and began laying the groundwork for their program of delivering the Synod from what they said was the rampant false doctrine poisoning its seminaries, teachers' colleges, and mission departments. At that Grace meeting with Walter Christopher, I sensed for the first time the early warning signs that the controversy that had split the meeting in Denver down the middle would not leave Grace Church untouched, because a few voices spoke favorably of the new leadership. But the majority of Grace members hoped for the best in spite of it and welcomed my announcement that the neighboring American Lutheran Church pastor and I would exchange pulpits in a few weeks.

The joy of expanded Lutheran fellowship ties, however, was soon tempered by news that the new Synod president had summarily sacked Dr. Richard Jungkuntz, his former faculty colleague at Springfield and currently chairman of the Synod's Commission on Theology and Church Relations. I heard of this in the spring of 1970, and it disturbed me that a gifted theologian was put out of a job with little more than a week's notice. I had learned of it via a report from a Michigan pastoral meeting that was letting its concern be known. Pastor Bertwin Frey had attended that meeting from his suburban Cleveland parish and had called for the support of Jungkuntz and his family, as well as realism regarding what was afoot in the church body. Frey and I communicated by phone and letter about those matters, and we agreed to do two things: we would write as many clergy as we knew, appealing for immediate support for Jungkuntz's salary as a summer school professor at Concordia Seminary, St. Louis; we would include in the same mailing a statement I had written that called for LCMS clergy support of an appeal for pastoral rather than bare-knuckled leadership from Jacob Preus. Remembering Otto Geiseman's example of garnering the support of Grace Church for his prophetic role in 1945, I brought these plans and the support statement to Grace's elders before acting on them. Our people not only approved the Jungkuntz support fund but opened Grace Church as a channel for Professor Jungkuntz and his family. It also heartened me that we gathered 1,215 signatures to the statement on short notice, representing approximately 20 percent of the Missouri Synod's clergy roster. With no intention at the time for anything beyond emergency help for a stranded brother, our action of gathering signatures and support gave birth to the Frey-Lueking network, an endeavor that had varying degrees of success and failure in the rocky evangelical cause within the Synod for the next half dozen years.

On a May morning in 1970, Bert Frey and I got on a plane headed for St. Louis to present our appeal personally to President Preus. Knowing his sense of the political, we brought the 1,215 signatures with us to make our visit more purposeful. He heard us out, but he did not respond to our appeal for Jungkuntz or for more even-handed presidential leadership. Instead, he proposed that we return in a week to present our materials to the LCMS's Board of Directors, ignoring our objective of simply asking him to take the appeal seriously himself and do with it whatever he would. Also, we were traveling at our own expense and on time that was taken from busy parish ministries. But we returned as he requested.

The meeting with the Board of Directors that next week was a disaster. The seating arrangement in the room told us where we stood — or sat — with the leadership present: Preus and the board members sat around a large table; Frey and Lueking sat outside the circle, which meant that we stared at the backs of the heads of those to whom we were asked to speak. Preus himself began the session with an angry harangue that accused us of undermining his leadership, and an out-of-hand rejection of our appeal for fraternal treatment of respected theologians in positions of important responsibility. Then followed an obviously rehearsed litany of speeches by the board members supporting the president and sharply criticizing us. Unbeknownst to me or Frey, Preus and each board member had in hand a file of my personal letters and memos. I felt as though I was in the presence of CIA operatives rather than brethren in the faith. Later I found out that, without my knowledge or consent, my church secretary had sent my personal files first to Robert Preus, who then made sure they reached his brother, Jacob. When I asked her if this was true, her answer was to resign on the spot and never set foot in Grace Church again.

This turn of events gave me a jolt but left me wiser about what I was getting into and the tactics to which the new leadership would stoop. Not only was I wiser, but the leadership of Grace was less naïve as well. As much as I was resolved not to involve the congregation in a church fight that would only get worse, I could not shield the parish from these realities. The controversy would not go away. It was already the subject of national news coverage, and the several thousand clergy with whom Frey and I would be in contact looked to us to continue to advocate the evangelical theology that had nurtured us in congregations of our youth, in our seminary years at Concordia, St. Louis, and now in our parish ministries across the land. Other pastors in the Synod began to make similar efforts of protest; and the list lengthened of professors, synodical staffers, and missionaries who left their ministries because of harassment or who were simply terminated without cause. Pastors Richard Koenig of Amherst, Massachusetts, and Omar Stuenkel of Cleveland were among those active in protest. None of us relished these activities or saw ourselves as political kingmakers in the Synod. The near total dominance of the far right-wing political machinery made the claims that we wanted to "take over" the Synod laughable. We were all up to our ears in the daily work of parish ministry, thoroughly inept at countering the Preus juggernaut, and, besides, without the killer instinct necessary for such a quixotic venture. More to the point, in late 1970 and early 1971 the majority of Grace parishioners had no stomach for a full diet of what St. Paul called "stupid controversies, dissensions, and futile quarrels" (Titus 3:9). I was not about to force-feed them.

Later in 1971, however, a shock wave went right through our congregation: one of our most esteemed parishioners, Dr. Ralph Gehrke, came under the charge of teaching false doctrine at Concordia Teachers College, River Forest, where he was chairman of the religion department. Since joining Grace Church in 1962, Gehrke had taught hundreds of our parishioners in Sunday morning Bible classes and Sunday afternoon seminars, raising our adult education to new heights. The charges against Gehrke were as ironic as they were troubling, since he was well known at Grace as a man of deep faith, an effective teacher and biblical scholar, and one who was transparently Christ-like in his gentle manner. The accuser was a pastor from a nearby suburb who had collected student notes from Gehrke's classroom lectures for years as evidence against him — without ever going to Gehrke himself. The basis of his charge of false doctrine was the fundamentalist standard of a literal interpretation of every detail in Genesis 1–3 and 5–11, as well as an insistence that the 66 chapters of the Book of Isaiah had to be the work of one author.

Gehrke believed and taught that the entire Bible is the inspired Word of God and authoritative for faith and life. He was enough of a scholar to recognize that the Holy Spirit used different modes of literary form to convey the central message of sin and grace. But the accusation against him disregarded his reverence for *what* Scripture revealed by insisting on a non-Lutheran concept of *how* Scripture was given. The key word was a non-Lutheran term about the Bible, *inerrancy*. It worked like this: if one does not believe that the snake actually talked to Adam in the Garden, that Noah lived 930 years, that Jonah was in the belly of the great fish for three days, then one undercuts the truth of the gospel and the power of God for life and salvation. The accusations against Gehrke were dumbed down to: "he doesn't believe the Bible"; he teaches that the Bible is full of errors; he denies the inspiration of the Bible and thus destroys faith. During the eight years of defending himself against these charges, Gehrke was consistently cleared by Martin Koehneke, his president at Concordia College, as well as the school's Board of Control, which has authority in such matters. That did not matter to the accuser, who kept coming at him until, two years later, a new president and new board of control arrived at Concordia College with the Preus stamp of approval for reopening the case against Gehrke. This struck me and many at Grace as a flagrant breach of every canon of fair procedure in secular jurisprudence, not to mention the covenantal bond of faith and brotherly love one would expect among Christians.

What I learned from the campaign against Gehrke was that there was little or no theology involved; this was about power politics, control through organizational leverage, and the relentless harassment of those who did not toe the party line. And as similar outrages descended on other faithful people in the Missouri Synod, I also learned not to underestimate the demonic character of a church fight. Now the people of Grace Lutheran Church would have the unwelcome occasion to experience firsthand the sin of bringing down a gifted teacher of the church and fellow parishioner who came as close to the biblical picture of saint as most of us would have the privilege of knowing.

A new tool that could be used against Gehrke and his counterparts in faculties of the synodical seminaries and colleges appeared at the Missouri Synod's 1971 convention in Milwaukee. Arthur Wellman and I were the lay and pastoral delegates from Grace Church, and I recall being deeply moved, with no embarrassment for my tears, by the message to the convention from the young Kent Knutson, president of the American Lutheran Church. It was far more than a perfunctory greeting from a church bureaucrat. His plea for depth and genuineness in making the act of pulpit and altar fellowship a channel of the Spirit for a whole new era of ministry was a thrilling call to rise above squabbles and catch the vision of Christ Jesus filling his church with power and vision. From this opening burst of inspiration, the rest of the convention was a downward spiral into the obvious or the irrelevant. The low point was Jacob Preus's angry tirade against all of us who opposed him as he sought to make a six-page document he had written the definitive standard for resolving alleged false doctrine. I knew we had not seen the last of the Preus statement; indeed, it would reappear two years later with consequences that split the Synod.

Meanwhile, Ralph Gehrke continued to teach adult Bible classes at Grace with great benefit to the members, especially a series on the Savior's resurrection according to the New Testament Gospels and another on God's mission to the world based on the book of Isaiah. This was what was so confounding: while the synodical leadership was accusing him of destroying the Bible, Grace members were fed abundantly by his biblical teaching. Among the best fellowships in the Word that we have known at Grace were the Sunday afternoon seminars Gehrke led, with teaching from 4:00 to 5:30, then a potluck supper, then continued study until 8:00, closing with vespers. These were welcome, needed hours for a core of sixty or more parishioners; we found them refreshing and faith-building and one more experience of the gift this man was to the parish and church at large. As the charges against him did not let up, I asked him to meet with our church council personally, as well as to explain his dilemma at meetings open to the entire congregation. We were acquiring, though reluctantly by many who had deep loyalties to the Synod, an education in how a denomination, as a human, fallible construct, is capable of becoming an obstacle to rather than a channel of the gospel. As Gehrke's pastor, I drew up a statement that both supported his sound biblical theology and sought to inform our members on what was at stake for us and the Synod in his ordeal.

The tide against Gehrke took a new turn in 1973 with the arrival of Dr. Paul Zimmerman as the new president of Concordia College. Several months before his departure into retirement, President Martin

Koehneke had called me to his home. This strong, buoyant man was slumped down on the sofa in his living room, head in his hands, dissolved in tears as he spoke of the toll of trying to administer a college faculty and student body under the siege of suspicion and accusation that had worn him down alarmingly. I had known him as a tower of strength under all the expectable tensions of being a college president. But the constant hammering against the faith and integrity of those faculty members he had brought to Concordia had left its mark, and I wondered whether those who saw themselves as restorers of pure doctrine had any idea of the pure havoc they were wreaking on the delicate handiwork of the Spirit in people such as Koehneke. The Concordia faculty committee on presidential candidates had submitted its preferences for the slate from which the presidents of the Synod and the local district and one other official would do the choosing. They ignored the work of the most senior members of the Concordia faculty, all of them Grace Church parishioners, and named Zimmerman to the position. He had taken an active role in bringing Preus to office, and they had been colleagues in earlier days at Bethany College in Mankato, Minnesota, a school of the ultraconservative wing of the Norwegian Lutherans. Soon after his arrival at Concordia, Zimmerman took the position that all previous statements of the Concordia administration and board affirming Gehrke's soundness as a Lutheran scholar and teacher of Scripture were null and void. Under the rubric of "clearing up the matter conclusively," Zimmerman not only accepted the charges against Gehrke as holding merit but expanded them with allegations of his own after conferring with his religion department chairman.

St. Paul cites the purpose of fraternal dialogue as speaking the truth in love with the goal of building each other up in the Body of Christ (Eph. 4:15ff.). The outcome of Zimmerman's action was to require that Ralph Gehrke stand trial on charges of false doctrine, charges that had now been expanded by his own president. What exasperated Gehrke to no end was the repeated injustice of not allowing him to voice *his own* expressions of faith in Christ and insight into God's Word; rather, they were being rephrased in summaries that Zimmerman provided to the board, now swung to an ultraconservative majority by the previous synodical convention. The board's decision came as no surprise to me; it was one more strike against a parishioner who had been hounded by fourteen years of harassment. My pastoral ministry to Gehrke during the years from 1969 through 1972 gave me and the congregation a sobering clarity about what was happening in the church body that had been Grace's home since its birth in 1902. At no time up to this point, however, had I given serious thought to the congregation's withdrawal from the Synod. In 1973 a painful, protracted process began that would change my mind.

At the July 1973 convention in New Orleans, the Missouri Synod made two decisions, this time by no means contradictory but fully consistent with the vision Preus and his supporters had had for the church body from his first day in office four years earlier. After heated debate among the more than one thousand delegates in a convention hall the size of a major league baseball park, by a vote of 562-455, Preus's "Statement on Scripture and Confessional Principles" was elevated to the status of a doctrinal statement that was to be binding on all members of the Lutheran Church–Missouri Synod. Shortly after that, by a 55-45 percent vote, the delegates placed forty-eight of the fifty-five members of Concordia Seminary, St. Louis, under the judgment of teaching false doctrine and being unfit for the church of God. Testing faithfulness was now determined by the political process of a majority vote by a stacked convention. The Preus people would categorically disagree with that conclusion, asserting that the Synod was only applying legitimate theological medicine to heal and unify a sick church body. My experience at the New Orleans convention, ten days filled with more pain and tears for my denominational household than I had ever known, was pinpointed by Concordia Seminary President John Tietjen's impassioned testimony to the assembly — and its rejection:

> I stand before you as a brother in the faith, a baptized child of God. I acknowledge that my life comes to me from God, the Creator, and that indeed He has made me and everything that is. I affirm before you that Jesus Christ is God and man, born of the

Virgin Mary, our Savior and Lord who gave his life in atonement for the sins of the world and was raised again for our justification. I affirm before you that I have been called to this faith not by my reason but by the Holy Spirit and that I live by the forgiveness of sins which I receive daily through the means of grace, the preaching of the Word and the administration of the sacraments, and together with all of you I look for the coming of our Lord Jesus Christ and our life together with Him in resurrection in heaven.

It was not enough for Tietjen to speak his heartfelt affirmation of the core of the biblical faith as witnessed by the confessional writings of the Lutheran church. This went unheard by those conditioned by reams of slanderous misrepresentation of his theological integrity and that of his faculty colleagues at Concordia Seminary. The impact of this witch hunt (I had no other term for it) by those acting as if the Eighth Commandment never existed made me face what I neither wanted to face nor thought I would ever have to face: the Synod leadership was by the tactics of unvarnished political power affirming what Martin Luther stood against at the Diet of Worms, the repression of the gospel and the testimony of the conscience. The shabbiness of the politicizing of the Missouri Synod before and during the New Orleans convention was a mirror image of Washington politics at that time and the Watergate tactics that traded on stolen documents (which I had experienced personally) and secret files against opponents (I once spotted a Preus supporter hiding behind a tree after photographing some of us exiting a meeting near Grace Church).

As for the effectiveness of the Frey-Lueking network at the convention, in which the other side elected 99 percent of its candidates to synodical offices, we were joint recipients of the George McGovern Political Achievement Award: its symbol was a long, sharply pointed shaft. As Richard Caemmerer reminded us, in New Orleans we lost everything but our sense of humor. That welcome light touch notwithstanding, the two crucial decisions of the convention concerning the Preus statement and the seminary made me think some new thoughts. The present leadership was changing my denominational home; the wrenching maltreatment of faithful, gifted teachers at Concordia Seminary forced me to face with realism the prospect of no longer being able to call it home. It was silencing the gospel by ignoring and then deposing my spiritual fathers and brothers who believed, taught, and confessed its saving power.

Coming home from the convention, I wondered how to translate it all to the parish. Walter Christopher was a delegate who had experienced it firsthand, as did his wife, Maxine, who accompanied him to the sessions. A half dozen other Grace people who were advisory delegates from Concordia College were there as well. They would all prove helpful. But finally it fell to me to tell the sad story, and I was at a loss as to how to do it. I decided that preaching the gospel to this situation was the faithful thing required of me. On the second Sunday after my return, I chose Romans 10:10 as my text (". . . for one believes with the heart and so is justified, and one confesses with the mouth and so is saved"). I began that sermon by looking full into the faces of the people so close to my heart and doing what the text says to do: I confessed with my mouth what I believed in my heart:

> I believe in the living God, who brought all things into being from nothing and sustains my life and yours to this moment. His miraculous power of creating is evident in the birth of my children and yours, and in the countless ways he surrounds me with providential love in daily life. I believe that in all things he is at work bringing good out of evil, for he has shown this supremely by sending his beloved Son, Jesus Christ our Lord, into our fallen world to rescue me and all mankind from sin. I believe that Jesus is Lord, his birth of the Virgin Mary, his life of ministry and miracles, came to fulfillment in his atoning death upon the cross and his glorious resurrection and ascension. I believe the good news of God's grace for me in Christ, because He has sent the Holy Spirit to dwell in my heart through the proclaimed Word of forgiveness and in the sacraments of Holy Baptism and Holy Communion. I believe that my purpose in life as a pastor, husband, father, and citizen is motivated by Christ's love for me. I gladly affirm the Holy Scriptures as God's written Word to me and to you, and with Christians of all time and

place look forward to the resurrection of my body and life eternal with the whole company of heaven.

This testimony to you from my heart is not made or measured by human decisions that seek to bind my soul and conscience; it is the testimony of the Holy Spirit within my spirit, who has been at work in my heart since my baptism forty-five years ago. Human efforts to regulate my faith and pastoral calling cannot penetrate to the deepest reaches of my being, which this text calls "the heart."

This heart of mine has something to say to you today. From my heart I tell you that the key decisions of our Synod's recent convention in New Orleans run head-on into the truth of this text and the deepest convictions we hold as Lutheran Christians. By a 562-455 vote, the delegates declared President Preus's "Statement of Scriptural and Confessional Principles" binding on the consciences of all of us. From my heart I tell you that this is wrong. . . . It is right for delegates to synodical conventions to make every effort to admonish, reprove, encourage, and edify each other by speaking the truth in love. But it is wrong — disastrously wrong — for synodical convention delegates to assume that a majority vote makes a resolution on doctrine binding on the conscience of anybody. It is wrong because God's Word alone, not man's, can bind the conscience, the soul, the very heart and inner being of a Christian. It is wrong because the action of making convention resolutions on doctrine binding sets us on the path to sectarianism ("we alone have the full truth") and derails us from the course Lutherans are called to follow as a confessional movement within the mainstream of Christianity. . . .

This fiasco has happened because there has been no open and honest airing of doctrinal issues among clergy, laity, and leaders. Good Christian people have been mailed a steady stream of biased, judgmental, loveless literature that only misleads; I name them before you: "Christian News" and "Affirm." Faithful professors who teach our seminarians at Concordia, St. Louis, have been branded as teachers of false doctrine. For the past four years the administration of the Synod under Jacob Preus, instead of providing a fair and honorable arena for the airing of differences, has led the attack against brothers. . . . I cannot and will not judge their hearts. But I can and must declare my heart's testimony that these actions are wrong and sinful. . . . I can understand the anguish others feel over the divided Synod in which we are called to walk together, and the impulse to settle things for good by political means. But we must stand under the Word. The way to solve our difficulties is not wrangling about the Word but getting into it together and staying under the power of the gospel until we agree! That hearing and doing the Word can bring blessing only as it takes place in the spirit of Christ-like love and mutual trust. . . .

What is to be done now? First, we must not capitulate to fear nor fail as a congregation — laity as well as clergy — to face with guts and grace the raw power that seeks to control us and our church body. Second, we must not give in to the temptation to walk away from this whole mess in disgust, with no heart or practical support for those judged and expelled from their ministries. Third, in our congregation we shall promptly find the proper public forums for an open and fair understanding of what is at issue and what it means for our future. Do not shun these coming meetings; they will not be shouting matches or bickering contests, but by God's grace will challenge you to grow toward a more mature faith. Fourth, do not withhold your support of our Synod's faithful brothers and sisters serving here and abroad, whose ministries must not melt away under the heat of present controversies. Fifth, I ask our young men now at Concordia Seminary or considering the call to ministry not to lose heart but to continue to learn under that faculty, which is second to none in our land. Sixth, I ask you to support with prayer and money any brother who is expelled from his post of ministry because of the Preus Statement, which we shall study together in the coming weeks. How this support can be channeled is not yet clear, but we will find a way. We will not abandon men and women who are precious gifts of the Lord Jesus to our Synod.

These closing words from T. S. Eliot offer a timely poignancy as they point us beyond winning and losing in the hard days ahead for us:

> "If we take the widest view of a Cause, there is no such
>   thing as a lost Cause
> Because there is no such thing as a Gained Cause.
> We fight for lost causes because we know that our
>   defeat and dismay
> May be the preface to our successor's victory,
> Though our victory in itself may be temporary;
> We fight rather to keep something alive
> Than in expectation that anything will triumph."

This, dear Christians of Grace, is what we fight for, to keep something alive, the testimony of the heart.

As with my sermon protesting our involvement in Vietnam four years earlier, this one evoked no neutral response. Many received it warmly, others with caution, and a few with visible anger. A pro-Preus faction had been forming within the congregation, as I had particular occasion to notice a few months before the New Orleans experience. The March voters' meeting was the usual gathering of perhaps two dozen men to conduct parish business. This time it included a recommendation by the nominating committee that Oswald Hoffman, the Lutheran Hour preacher, be Grace's nominee for the Missouri Synod presidency. But a number of the pro-Preus members had made phone calls to others of their persuasion that they should join the voting assembly that evening. And so by a 14-13 vote, Jacob Preus became Grace Church's nomination for Synod president over Hoffman.

It astonished me that the next morning — and for several days thereafter — my phone rang with calls from religion editors of daily newspapers in Chicago, Milwaukee, Minneapolis, St. Louis, and Los Angeles, all wanting to confirm that the "Lueking parish" (a term I detested) had in fact nominated Preus. That told me two things: Grace was not of one mind in the synodical struggle; and our church was living in a fishbowl of national attention because of the Frey-Lueking efforts. The following Sunday, Oswald Hoffman was the homilist for our Bach Cantata Vesper and treated the matter with his infectious cackle instead of any gnashing of teeth. Subsequent gloating in right-wing publications of the Synod was forthcoming as sure as the sunrise; I answered the letters of consolation with the Hoffmanesque touch of humor. But there was one lasting result: from that time forward, every voters' meeting at Grace was attended by between 100 and 300 people. The aroused congregational awareness of our bellwether status gave me headaches as well as satisfaction. I established the policy of channeling the synodical issue discussion and debate into the voters' meetings or special meetings for all members and did not use my pastoral letter as a bully pulpit.

A minority (pro-Preus) faction sought the parish list to disseminate their version of things, which the church council refused on the basis that everybody could speak and listen in sessions designed for that purpose. The group sent letters out anyway, at first anonymously and then with one or several signers. These were aimed at me and my leadership at Grace Church and in the community at large, and they grew longer and more shrill as the controversy dragged on. I trusted the people of Grace to judge the claims on their merits, and though these letters were an annoyance, only once did I become really angry: that was when a letter making the rounds claimed the Geiseman legacy at Grace for the Preus cause and accused me of betraying that legacy. The elders calmed me down by reminding me of the wisdom of never trying to get even in public. I let them handle me and my anger, which was not worth the emotional energy it could have cost me and the parish, which would realize no benefit from overkill by me or those after my jugular.

In the autumn of 1973, I led a series of study sessions on the Preus Statement and appointed a panel of three parishioners who were on the Concordia faculty to join me in presenting as balanced a study of the document as possible. Dr. Paul Kreiss was the leader of the group within Grace that supported the Preus Statement; Professors Dan Poellet and Kenneth Heinitz were known and respected as belonging to no political camp. Where I stood was well enough known. What was evident from the very first, and throughout the continuing sessions, was the divisiveness of the document. We could not get into the document without acrimony over its content and its purpose as a binding tool discerning truth from falsehood. My way of communicating that to the Grace parishioners was to compare the denominational conflict to a troubled marriage. It makes matters worse if an additional requirement is added to the marriage vows of loving, honoring, and cherishing each other — an add-on phrase implying that those three are not enough. Similarly, Holy Scripture, the three ecumenical creeds, and the Lutheran Confession do not need the add-on of the Preus Statement to determine sound Lutheran doctrine and practice. And making it binding seals in the conflict.

Those sessions were not productive: our members sensed its transparently arid and sectarian spirit, its use as a Sword of Damocles over faculty and churchmen in St. Louis. Despite the national publicity attending the majority of faculty and students of Concordia Seminary when they marched off the campus to form Concordia Seminary in Exile, housed temporarily by the Jesuits of St. Louis University, that dramatic result of their condemnation by the New Orleans convention was miles away from Grace Church. Though John Tietjen had addressed our parish personally in a moving presentation of his struggle and dilemma, he was an admired churchman who lived and taught elsewhere. Even though a missionary educator who was a close friend of and coworker with Otto Geiseman in earlier synodical causes, Dr. Thomas Coates, was cut off from support in his seminary post in Hong Kong (and fully supported by Grace Church from 1977 through 1979), he was half a world away. When Grace parishioner and promising church historian Dr. John Groh was dismissed from the Concordia College faculty without cause, Grace Church called him to our pastoral staff and posted him on the Concordia Seminary in Exile faculty (with Grace support); still, he and his family were now in St. Louis and we were here. All of these actions had come as forms of response to my sermon following the New Orleans convention, and each of them was resisted by an increasingly dug-in minority group within the congregation. As significant as each action was, and as grateful as I was for the courage of the congregation in offering spiritual and material support, these did

not have the same impact as the continuing struggle of our own parishioner, Ralph Gehrke.

In the spring of 1975, the elders invited Professor Gehrke to present
his response to the charges against him in a special meeting open to all
members. Several hundred members filled the Fellowship Hall to listen,
often in disbelief, as this seasoned teacher of the Word spoke his response to the charges against him. In one sense it was unthinkable that
Gehrke should have to make such a defense. But in another way it was a
splendid moment for the congregation and its accused member.
Gehrke, ever the teacher, turned it into a learning experience, not only
in deepening our grasp of the many and varied ways God has spoken
through the prophets and now in these last days through the Christ, but
also in making clear the demonic things that happen to Christians *because* they stand in the power of the Word when under fire. His unambiguous commitment to the cardinal Lutheran principles of faith alone
and grace alone in believing, teaching, and confessing the gospel made
him a living sign of what Luther called the theology of the cross, which
means holding fast to God not in the nakedness of his glory but knowing him through the wounds of the suffering Christ. Gehrke's witness
was not an exercise in self-justification but a demonstration of the
power of the Word that had sustained him through a dozen years of relentless accusation aimed at bringing him down by any means. That evening inspired a move within the congregation to prepare a testimony of
affirmation of Gehrke's soundness in faith and teaching. I wrote a brief
document for that purpose, which was signed by parishioners. A group
of Concordia colleagues contacted over three hundred of Gehrke's former students, who then wrote testimonial letters in behalf of their
teacher. These were submitted to the Concordia president and board of
control and others who were interested. Gehrke was heartened by this
support as the day of his trial approached, the first Saturday in June
1977.

I sat with him as his pastor during his trial, which was held in a
meeting room of a motel near O'Hare International Airport. The day,
which began at 9 a.m. and ended at 7 p.m., was an exhausting, dismal experience, the polar opposite of the Ephesians 4 picture of believers con-

tending for the truth together — no longer as children tossed this way and that by every wind of doctrine and human trickery, but growing into the full stature of Christ by speaking the truth in love. Given the makeup of the panel of judges, all long on synodical loyalty but short on an understanding of biblical theology, their finding that Gehrke was guilty of teaching false doctrine came as no surprise. Their measure of determining fitness for sound teaching was not the confessional writings of the Lutheran tradition but the Preus Statement, and by that standard his repeated witness to the authority of the Word as defined by its evangelical center was irrelevant. Both Gehrke and I felt emptied out after ten hours of fruitless grilling and in need of the haven of a home. Gehrke, a man well established in his single vocation, accepted my invitation to come to our family table, where he was still able to greet Beverly and our children with good cheer despite the day he had just endured.

This day brought to a head a process that had begun a half dozen years earlier, my reluctant conviction that my future was not in this church body. A year later, Dr. Gehrke was formally expelled from the Lutheran Church–Missouri Synod. The final act of the fifteen-year-long ordeal was a one-sentence letter from the district president informing him, "Your name has been removed from the clergy roster." This was not the end of Ralph Gehrke's teaching vocation in the church: he went on to become the head of the religion department at Pacific Lutheran University in Tacoma, Washington, and to teach for shorter periods in seminaries of the Far East and in Papua New Guinea. We felt his loss at Grace Church; it certainly left a deep imprint on me as his pastor. In looking back on our congregational experiences with the synodical leadership from 1969 through 1977, I saw the cumulative effect of the accusations, judgment, trial, and expulsion of Ralph Gehrke as a microcosm of such compelling clarity of what had overtaken the Synod that in my judgment it was the determinative factor in our withdrawal from the Synod. We had something better to do than stay in and fight. Seven years of trying had made that clear. Our calling was to keep something alive among us, the gospel and the free course of ministry that grows from it — and we needed to be kept alive by it.

A welter of events filled the summer months of 1977, prior to the parish decision regarding our relationship with the Synod. In June a graduate of Concordia Seminary in Exile, now known as Seminex, was called to become our assistant pastor. Aaron Sorrels was a son of Grace Church and brought a well-tested maturity to his work with us. This call was stoutly opposed by the minority pro-Preus group, who tried to prevent it by a civil court injunction as late as the day before Sorrels's ordination. Following his ordination, the more strident among them scorned his ordination vows by conspicuously referring to him as Mister Sorrels, never Pastor Sorrels. A more offensive slur against him and all his fellow Seminex graduates was made by Jacob Preus himself, who asked a Florida audience if they wanted graduates "from an illegal seminary to be making calls on housewives when they are home alone." Prior to his ordination, two elders and I had flown to St. Louis to argue the relevance of a deep-rooted Missouri Synod tradition, that the calling of pastors is centered in the autonomy of the congregation. We rejected the Preus administration's demand that Sorrels first submit to a colloquy, arguing that two hours of interview by a biased committee was intolerable as a validation of five years of theological training.

A year earlier we had taken Dr. James Childs onto Grace Church's staff as a part-time theologian-in-residence after he and his faculty colleagues at Concordia Senior College, Fort Wayne, had been ousted by a single stroke of the prior synodical convention: the Preus administration's dismantling of the entire pre-seminary educational structure of the Synod. From the fall of 1976 through the spring of 1977, Childs spent twenty hours a week in on-site job visits with several dozen selected parishioners. Of primary importance during the spring of 1977 were three all-member meetings dealing with the practical matters of how we would proceed as an independent congregation, organizationally speaking, while still interdependent with the wider Lutheran mission, benevolence, and educational ministries. The Fellowship Hall was packed for these meetings — up to 400 members present for each. The March meeting featured, among other topics, presentations by Walter Christopher and Gerald Koenig on staff coverage for medical insurance and pensions (the Missouri Synod people responsible in these areas were consistently helpful, courteous, and efficient in all our contacts with them). The April meeting focused on theological issues: our invited guest, President Edmund Happel of the local synodical district, emphasized loyalty to the denomination as the remedy for the theological issues that were tearing us apart. But the speech that probably had the most impact among the responses from the floor that evening was a three-liner by veteran member Milton Tatter, a plain-spoken plumber who arose to say: "Dr. Geiseman said, 'You watch out for those boys in St. Louis because if they ever get their fingers in the affairs of Grace Church you'll be lost.' It sounds like we're up against a hierarchy like the Catholic Church. There's a new little Vatican in St. Louis."

I know when words touch a responsive chord by the sheer strength of their simplicity; that was just such an occasion. In May, I presented my vision of our parish future under the heading of five goals: (1) recalling our parish tradition of contending for a gospel-centered way of church life; (2) sound Lutheran and not sectarian footing for our ministry as people and pastor; (3) the intention to sustain and widen fellowship with other Lutherans; (4) the commitment to mission to the community and world without continued embroilment in church controversy; and (5) the prime importance of regular worship as the source that holds us together in God's love. The quality of preparation for and participation in those three meetings, together with the size of attendance that held up throughout, gave me the sense of fulfilling my pastoral leadership responsibilities as best I could in anticipation of the major decision that was coming. Everyone was free to speak. The Synod's official voice was heard. Hard questions were asked and answered openly, including those acknowledging that the future was by no means risk-free — one risk being that of losing our building and property to the Synod.

During July 1977, I traveled to Los Angeles for meetings with clergy and laity among the 100,000-plus members of the six hundred or so congregations that had left the Missouri Synod for an interim organization until the Association of Evangelical Lutheran Churches was formed. I had participated in the formation of Evangelical Lutherans in Mission (ELIM) during the heady days of 1973 and following, when pioneering new forms of theological education at Seminex and new structures for overseas and U.S. mission work kept me in frequent contact with like-minded others throughout the nation. Another major task for me during that summer of 1977 was working with the church council on a recommendation for the September voters' meeting and the decision to withdraw from the Synod. Every word of that document had to be precise in stating the theological grounds for an action of this scope, how it would affect our congregation and school ministry and mission, and what we needed to understand about what legal implications our leaving the Synod would have for the continued ownership of our property. By the evening of September 20, 1977, we were prepared.

Those who were present that evening at Grace Church will not forget the sight and feeling of some 800 people gathered in the sanctuary, some of them collegians who had traveled several hundred miles to cast their vote for a future they cared about. The number who were eligible to vote was closer to 650. The rest were friends of the congregation and former members who had come back to witness what they sensed would be a historic evening. I had skipped the supper hour at home with Beverly and the children, instead spending it hunched over my typewriter, working and reworking the brief pastoral message I was to deliver. My closest friend, Martin Marty, popped in for a handshake and a word of encouragement. He was soon followed by Marvin Dumler, a large man of unflappable disposition and unquestioned integrity, ideal for his role as chairman of the meeting. We reviewed the format.

Shortly before 8 p.m. all was in order, and I walked into the sanctuary, moving up and down the center aisle amidst the buzz of conversation but no laughter, greeting people with a nod or handshake but no small talk. Some of the faces did not turn my way; others were set in anger. I accepted the fact that people needed a focus for their sinking feelings that whatever hope they harbored for keeping the status quo was slipping away. The faces reflecting upset and irritation gave me reason to realize how short our memories are. One of those present who turned her face away, unable to accept my hand of greeting, had suffered terrible burns in a home fire several years before; in repeated pastoral visits to her during the long, painful recovery I had not remembered her turning her face away. But that was then and this was now. The thought of her congregation as no longer a part of the Missouri Synod she had known all her life made her lose her manners, momentarily at least. She had not the slightest idea of the issues. My love for her was no less, even when she stared straight ahead and said, "I wish I had died instead of living to see this evening." Her sister gave her a gentle chiding, sparing me a regretful look her way.

The meeting began with prayer. The first matter on the agenda was to determine how long each person could speak. "Two minutes," Dave Moeller proposed. Wilfred Kruse, whose granite-like fairness, intelligence, and droll sense of humor had blessed the parish for a half-century, countered with the plea that we all should be ready to stay with it all night long if necessary. But the two-minute limit passed resoundingly, indicating the mood of people who had heard enough long speeches for three years and favored limits that would make everyone get directly to the point. I spoke my pastoral message first: I explained why we should leave, then called for respectful speaking and listening to each other, and sat down with time to spare on the two-minute clock. The recommendation was read: it recommended that, after several years of study and discussion related to the controversy in the Lutheran Church–Missouri Synod and its effect on the congregation, Grace Lutheran Church withdraw its membership effective October 1, 1977, and continue our mission and ministry as an independent Lutheran congregation according to the standards of faith set forth in Article II of the parish constitution. The proposal had been mailed to each address of the parish several weeks earlier and carried the signatures of the full church council of nineteen men and women, plus the senior staff of six, and included four pages of commentary.

One by one the speakers stepped to the microphone placed at the head of the chancel, a timekeeper alongside with a two-minute warning buzzer. Among the advocates for staying were none of the strident voices of sharp judgment that had been aimed primarily at me, which was politically astute. Among those favoring leaving were those who had borne the brunt of our journey and wanted not simply out but onward with our mission. After an hour and a half the speaking was done. The vote was taken by blind ballot to be placed in boxes at the head or the nave. As the procession of balloting began, I moved my folding chair up two steps from the sanctuary floor to the chancel so that I could better see the faces of these people, of whom I was immensely proud and to whom I was genuinely grateful — except for one hard-bitten nay-sayer who lifted the lid of the ballot box to see whether it had been stuffed beforehand. While the votes were counted, Paul Bouman went up to the organ bench and led us in a time of hearty, wonderful hymn-singing. Yet the singing of those sturdy chorales was tinged with an awareness of sadness that this might be the last time all of us would sing our faith together. No one made a move to leave. The tally was brought in and read: 425 to leave, 199 to stay. The motion had passed by better than two to one. We had taken the step. No cheers or jeers. A respectful quiet prevailed as the people filed out of the sanctuary at about 10:30. Beverly and I found our way home sometime later, tired but grateful that we could experience this evening with a congregation we both deeply loved and admired.

It was over — but, of course, it was not over. The Synod battle scene would now shift from congregational meetings in our Fellowship Hall to courtrooms in Chicago, Springfield, Illinois, and finally the United States Supreme Court in Washington.

CHAPTER 6

Ministry While Containing
a Court Battle

After you've done your best, pray for the forgiveness of
sins.

GEORGE FOREL

The contract Grace Church had signed fifty years before, in 1927, to buy
the River Forest property from the Missouri Synod contained three
clauses whereby the Synod could buy back the property and its improvements. The first two were straightforward: (1) repurchase by the Synod
could happen if Grace would decide to sell it, or (2) if Grace joined another church body not affiliated with the Synod. The third clause was
the stickler. It stated that the Synod could buy back the property and its
improvements "if Grace Church shall fail or decide not to teach and
preach the Scriptures as set forth under Article II entitled 'Confession'
of the constitution of the Missouri Synod and in accordance with the
rules, regulations, and customs of the Missouri Synod." Article II of the
Synod's constitution states this basis for its doctrine: "the canonical
books of the Old and New Testament as the inspired Word of God, and
the three Ecumenical Creeds and the symbolical books of the Lutheran

reformation as true and sound expositions of the faith." This is identical to the doctrinal basis stated in the Grace Church constitution, which, incidentally, mentions the Missouri Synod nowhere.

Already six months before our decision to leave, the Missouri Synod's lawyer in St. Louis had rendered an opinion that, by leaving the Synod, Grace Church would trigger the third clause of the contract. The message of a March 21, 1977, letter to the congregation was clear that, if we withdrew, the Synod would not only buy back the property but enforce the action in a civil court, if necessary. On behalf of the church council I wrote a response to what appeared to us as a threat, and I cited 1 Corinthians 6:1-8 as biblical grounds for our church bodies to stay out of the civil courts. On the face of it, the contract's clause holding us to the "rules, regulations, and customs of the Missouri Synod" in confessing Lutheran doctrine would seem to make it impossible for Grace to withdraw and assume independent status.

On closer examination, however, we found something wrong with their reading of the matter that appeared to us to be analogous to the claim that one could not play baseball unless one belonged to a certain league. Here was the point, stated unambiguously in Article VII of the Synod's constitution: "In its relation to its members Synod is not an ecclesiastical government exercising legislative or coercive powers, and with respect to the individual congregation's right of self-government it is but an advisory body. Accordingly, no resolution of Synod imposing anything upon the individual congregation is of binding power if it is not in accordance with the Word of God or if it appears to be inexpedient as far as the condition of the congregation is concerned." Since 1839, when the German immigrant colony had barely survived an imperious leader who tried to set up a Lutheran papacy in southeastern Missouri, the Synod had held fiercely to the autonomy of the local congregation. The advisory character of the Synod meant just that: its rules, regulations, and customs were advice, not canon law. Yet — and this is the irony of its history — the Synod was as close-knit in its customs and traditions as any immigrant group would be in a new land.

All this notwithstanding, in 1977 Grace Church came face to face with harsh evidence that the Synod had swung over to a hierarchical polity that defied its charter. The Synod's self-defined advisory character was nowhere in sight as it declared its determination to interpret our land contract in its own self-interests and force Grace Church to sell back our property. The legal issue involved here was twofold: the matter of interpreting the terms of a real estate contract and the issue of the advisory relationship between Synod and congregation. It was the latter issue that brought us national attention as the legal battle dragged on over the next eight years. Whether we liked it or not, we were a congregation squarely in the cross hairs of the synodical administration, a circumstance too juicy for the press to neglect. The most recent reminder of the national publicity we did not seek came on the night of our decision to withdraw: by midnight the Grace Church decision was an item on the religious news national wire service.

On October 1 (after that September 20 decision), the Missouri Synod Board of Directors informed us of its determination to purchase our property and buildings for $750,000. Two days later, President Paul Zimmerman of Concordia College called me to his office. Without comment, he handed me the proposal printed on a single page bearing the official seal of the Missouri Synod. I read it through and asked one question: How had the price been determined? He said that he did not know. It was good that I left his office without speaking another word. A fury was rising up in me at the arrogance of an uncontested claim to have the right to buy Grace Church and the insult of the price of $750,000. The most recent insurance estimate pegged the worth of the building at just over two million dollars. My walk back across the campus gave me a full view of the soaring magnificence of the Tower of Praise, as it was called, the visual symbol of all that Grace Church and School stood for. My mind turned back to the stories of the struggle and sacrifice that the Grace faithful had undergone to pay for the church during the Depression years, and yet their commitment never to miss their contribution to the support of the Synod throughout that time. In fact, Grace had led all congregations of the LCMS in a "Thank Offering" appeal just ten years earlier. Now I had in my hand a document from that Synod under leadership of a wholly different spirit. "Shabby and shameful" were the only words that came to me to characterize this effort to grab this jewel at bargain basement prices.

I had to move quickly beyond my emotions, however, to a clearer understanding of the legal process that had been set in motion by the Synod proposal. The original contract declared that if the option to buy was activated, both parties had thirty days to agree on the price. If a price could not be agreed on in thirty days, an arbitration process had to follow during the next sixty days. With its one-page document the Synod's board had declared its legal right to buy Grace Church and had named its price as step one of a legal process. The terms of the contract required us to inform them of our decision concerning their offer, and to do it within thirty days — with further negotiation to follow if no agreement was reached. If our response would be that their legal claim to buy was invalid and their price ridiculous, they would have us in court in St. Louis after the stipulated time had expired.

This assumption was confirmed by the attorney we had contacted during the spring of that year, William Theiss, of the Chicago firm of Kirkland and Ellis. Our own team of parish attorneys, Ken Hartmann, Martin Baumgaertner, Pat Allen, and Cliff Meacham, confirmed that opinion as well. Over the coming years these men would volunteer hundreds of hours of time without charge, a gift that kept our legal costs far below what they would have been otherwise. We realized early on that we needed to go outside the parish for a lead attorney who specialized in church-state law. Theiss suggested James Serritella, whose qualifications suited our needs well. His first assignment was to confer with the synodical attorney about a fair out-of-court settlement. A group of Missouri Synod leaders met with our elders and me in late October to seek such a solution. Their first suggestion was that the Grace members who voted to leave the Synod should contact the nearest American Lutheran Church congregation and move in with them. Their second proposal wasn't much better: that a panel of three Missouri Synod jurists be found who would consider the issues and make the final decision — with no right of appeal.

While we were rapidly losing confidence that the synodical representatives were serious about a fair settlement, another development added to our disillusionment. We learned that those representing the Missouri Synod were simultaneously conferring with a group of dissident Grace parishioners who had effectively withdrawn from our fellowship but were ready to declare in a civil court that, by opposing the vote to leave the Missouri Synod, they were the true Grace Church and that the property was legally theirs. This did not surprise me because, along with the majority of the congregation, I had endured their methods and way of thinking for several years. With no response from the Synod to our willingness to meet further on the land contract interpretation, with the thirty days soon to expire, and with the minority group poised to go to court with a claim to be the true Grace Church, we faced this dilemma: either the Synod would take us to court in St. Louis for breach of contract, or the minority group would take us to court in Chicago. We had no other choice but to take action ourselves.

On October 18, acting on our behalf by the authority of the church council, James Serritella filed for a declaratory judgment by the Circuit Court of Cook County, pleading that our action in leaving the Synod for independent status did not trigger the terms of the 1927 land contract. This was not a decision we reached lightly; the council members and I agonized over it. Six months earlier I had brought up to the Synod leadership St. Paul's injunction against Christians hauling each other into a civil court. I knew that the cry of hypocrisy would go up against us. But we had no reason to trust that the Synod's jerry-rigged panel of jurists would be capable of handling not only the technicalities of real estate law but also of adjudicating the larger and — for us — decisive issue of the advisory nature of the Synod-congregation relationship. Was it advisory or hierarchical? We knew of no precedent in the church body for solving a dilemma that was unique to our situation. The Missouri Synod had no religious court to handle real estate law. No land contract like ours existed anywhere else in the Synod. Was there case law that pertained to our situation? Was the fundamental matter of enforcing the accusations that we were not preaching Lutheran doctrine correctly even permissible in a civil court?

These factors pressed in on us during the first two weeks of October 1977, and pushed us to make the decision we made. With no illusions of perfection about ourselves, yet determined to protect an exceptional house of worship and school handed down to us by those who sacrificed greatly, we did the best we could. And then we asked for the forgiveness of our sins. No one goes through an ordeal like this untouched by the greatest temptation of all, the self-righteousness whereby we would portray ourselves as saints and the others as sinners. We were all stained by sin, and the eight-year struggle was just beginning.

Our position throughout was this: our leaving the Synod did not authorize the Missouri Synod to buy back our property; that the minority was not the true Grace Church; and that the First Amendment of the U.S. Constitution forbade a civil court to adjudicate whether Grace Church could preach and teach Lutheran doctrine correctly. This position held at every point from the Circuit Court of Cook County, through the appeals courts, to the Supreme Court of the State of Illinois, and finally to the the United States Supreme Court. It took eight years to reach the end of that court battle, which we did in May 1985. The legal costs to us in the first several years averaged $60,000 a year; but not one dollar for legal defense was taken from our funds of parish and mission support during that period, when our budget rose year by year. I have no idea of the cost to the Missouri Synod, which had no team of parish attorneys donating their time without fee. The eight-year process could have lasted less than a year had our opponents not appealed every decision. On the day the Supreme Court decision in our favor put an end to the struggle, I called the staff together to announce it, offer prayer, and sing a doxology of thanksgiving. There were no winners or losers. For us it was a matter of getting through it with our ministry intact and our parish united.

It was critically important to contain the legal battle and yet continue to concentrate on the main things for which we existed — worship and preaching, communing and baptizing, marrying and burying, ministering to the sick and homebound, and reaching out in mission. Throughout the decade and a half between 1970 and 1985, my chief goal was to keep the daily ministry of the gospel foremost and not to allow conflict to be a consuming obsession that would destroy the congregation. It was my pastoral responsibility to walk the fine line between keeping the parish my first priority while also finding a way to inform the members of the earthquake shaking the church body and putting our property at risk — about which they could, of course, read plenty in local and Chicago newspapers. I was imperfect in that responsibility, but I realized that it was essential to try, and along the way to listen to feedback from elders, staff, and parishioners. I needed their help in keeping my primary focus and best energies on four areas: preaching and worship, parish cohesion, mission outreach, and financial steward-ship.

In my preaching through those years, the cardinal rule I followed was to allow the prescribed biblical texts of the lectionary to set the course for week-by-week proclamation and teaching in sermons. Only rarely, when in my judgment the text called for it, did I refer to denominational prob-lems from the pulpit. My choice did not arise from fear or timidity, but from the desire to feed the people with what they came for. There were tumultuous things going on in the nation during those years as well, which formed a backdrop that set everyone's teeth on edge. It was the era of "dirty tricks," epitomized by the Watergate fiasco, the resignation of Richard Nixon, and the imprisonment of Spiro Agnew as well as key White House staff and other administration figures. The succession of these unprecedented crises sent a shudder of revulsion throughout the nation and congregation. Against that background, I knew that parish-ioners did not come to church for preaching that would rehash the syn-odical brouhaha as a mirror image of what was going on in Washington. I did not want preaching to echo the hard-line us-against-them divisive-ness that was so prevalent in the nation and the church in those times; it had to offer bread rather than stones. I welcomed the discipline of tex-tual preaching as my main means of faithfulness to God and the people he had called me to serve.

Regarding worship, a new publication of the Missouri Synod had appeared in 1971. *The Worship Supplement* was a start toward new litur-gies and hymns that, as its name implied, did not seek to replace the Lu-theran Hymnal but to supplement it. With so many of our own parish musicians involved in its preparation, there was ready acceptance at

Grace to begin using it that year on occasional Sundays. As we set out into the tricky waters of new liturgy and hymns, a first venture in pastoral leadership for me, I called on Paul Bouman's leadership to help avoid shipwreck. He in turn called in Carl Schalk to join him, before the worship service, in brief explanations of a manageable portion of the new liturgy and to coach the congregation in singing the new songs. This continued for a series of weeks, and for a half dozen years we used the old and new hymnals together with benefit. *The Lutheran Book of Worship* appeared in 1978, a joint Lutheran publication of all the major Lutheran bodies. Our member Richard Hillert wrote the major communion liturgy for the new *LBW,* and Carl Schalk and Paul Bunjes served as consultants during its preparation and wrote hymns that were included in it. We devoted a series of Sunday morning adult education classes to the *LBW* before introducing it and were fortunate to have Bouman, Schalk, and Hillert available as able presenters. As they had in 1971, the Bouman-Schalk team again went to work preparing the congregation with brief introductory explanations and practice before each Sunday service, which enabled parishioners to understand why we did what we did, when we did it, and how liturgy as a whole is the "work of the people." Their skill as teachers and their respect for the teachability of the parishioners blessed the congregation immeasurably; they did it with just the right combination of careful teaching, awareness of the range of musical ability among the members, and good-natured humor. Instead of making the acceptance of the *Lutheran Book of Worship* a march through a minefield, they made it something the parishioners welcomed as an opportunity to appreciate the wide stream of tradition as well as the gift of new contributions to it.

We also introduced the Easter Vigil during this period, which connected us to the most ancient liturgy of Christendom. From the first year we included it as the first service of Eastertide, I looked forward eagerly to joining those who were drawn to its sense of mystery and proclamation, of darkness and light, of silence and singing. The Paschal candle lit at the Vigil of Easter helped carry us throughout the six weeks of the Easter season and beyond to each baptism and funeral during the year. The three to four hours of readings, singing, baptisms, preaching, and the Eucharist were not tedious: together with the core of several hundred who came year after year, I loved the contrasts and continuities that helped keep "stupid controversies and futile wrangling" at a distance. Easter is my favorite season of the church year. The sight and sound of people whom I loved at worship never became routine through those weeks and months when I often felt that no one at Grace needed the buoyant power of worship more than I did.

I also became increasingly aware of how much Paul Bouman's partnership as music minister and teacher meant to me. Our weekly sessions to choose hymns and liturgies were more than routine planning meetings. His collegial spirit helped immensely in keeping worship primary in the life of the congregation — for their good as well as my own spiritual lifeline. Without that Sunday-by-Sunday oasis of prayer and preaching, sacrament and singing, the pressures of the 1970s would have drained me of the needed energy for and joy in my calling. In the decades since then, when I have occasionally been asked whether those years were nothing but awful, I can still answer that in all honesty I would not have missed them for anything. I can say that because, in facing tough dilemmas, it was worship with the congregation that was a richly restorative Sabbath refreshment for my weariness in body and soul.

In 1971 an idea long percolating in Paul Bouman's mind came to fulfillment. Well before coming to the Grace staff as minister of music as well as a teacher at Grace School, he had heard a teacher colleague and mentor in Milwaukee, Alfred Kowert, mention almost offhandedly that it was time for Lutherans in America to discover the treasure of the church music of J. S. Bach, particularly his cantatas written for every Sunday of the year. That brief comment did not fade from Bouman's memory, and in 1971 the opportunity came for him to act on it. He talked with Carl Schalk about starting a series of Bach Cantata Vespers at Grace Church. I was enthusiastic about the idea from its first mention and actively encouraged church members to lay the groundwork for what would be no small task. Their idea was for the Grace Choir and the Concordia Teachers College Choir to alternate months in singing a cantata as part of the Service of Evening Prayer, a liturgy ideally suited for the cantatas. My part was to secure preachers for each Vespers service and help raise money to pay the guest instrumentalists, soloists, and preachers.

The first Bach cantata went very well: our choir sang, and Richard Caemmerer of Concordia Seminary, St. Louis, preached. The series of eight cantatas a year began in a time when Bach was not widely sung in American congregations; to our knowledge, only Holy Trinity Lutheran Church in New York offered them regularly. At Grace it quickly established itself as an enduring tradition drawing people from throughout Chicago and beyond. A measure of its drawing power that impressed me was the sizable number of those who would rank a Bach cantata above the American Sunday afternoon religion of NFL football. Guest preachers of the caliber of Jaroslav Pelikan, Joseph Sittler, Oswald Hoffman, Herbert Lindemann, Kent Knutson, Paul Harms, and others, helped sustain the congregation's interest. Another help during those stressful years was the church supper after these Vesper services. I looked forward to those suppers as oases that kept me going for days afterward. Not only was my spirit warmed by the table fellowship and the stimulating dinner conversations with musicians and guest preachers, but the martini or glass of wine beforehand helped as well.

With respect to cohesion in the congregation through the 1970s, I welcomed every means available to strengthen the ties of belonging and sought new ways to help hold together 1,750 of us as a parish family. In 1971, I asked the elders and the Christian education committee to approve moving children's participation in communion from the confirmation age of fourteen to ten-year-olds. This came in conjunction with a church-wide study of confirmation and was readily accepted at Grace. Our arrangement brought together ten-year-old youngsters, their parents with them, for instruction immediately following the six Wednesday evening services in Lent. From the very first night I loved it. It tickled me to see the ten-year-olds run, not walk, from Lenten worship to the chapel, vie for space close to a friend, where each flopped down on the rug, checking to make sure their parents were seated close behind them. Their faces still eager in spite of the hour, they stayed with me for forty-five minutes of Bible history and catechism on the Sacrament of the Altar. When Holy Week came, and the children received their first communion, it was a high moment for them and their families — and all of us with them.

I was particularly keen to maintain our membership in those years, and I wanted no turning back from our theological direction because of our losses in membership. It was a poor motivation, to be sure, but it was real nonetheless. From 1971 onward, I added a summer schedule of adult instruction classes to the regular cycle of ten-week classes in fall and spring. I taught them myself for the most part; the hour between the 8:30 and 11 a.m. service was the best time for most inquirers to come, but it was not the best time for me. I had tried weeknight classes and even a series of Saturday late afternoon hours, followed by a potluck supper; but attendance was too uneven. The contact with people unfamiliar with Christian fundamentals of faith and life taught me as well as giving me an opportunity to teach; along with pastoral counseling, it was a way for me to measure the religious climate of our community — or the lack of it. What my method did not have was the inclusion of more testimony from the laity of Grace Church, ordinary people who could speak from their experience of what belonging to Christ meant for belonging to each other. That came in later years.

Our growth in adult instruction was never phenomenal at this or any time during my pastorate. The Lutheran tradition at its best leans more toward a depth of preparation rather than a breadth of numbers. This was certainly my experience at a time when disillusionment with institutions of all sorts was on the rise. We did take an active part in Key 73, a broad-based Protestant evangelism campaign in America in 1973. I was glad to have fifty pairs of our members sign on for several Saturdays of training at First Baptist Church in Oak Park. Our assignment was to canvass households in north River Forest for a church census of our neighborhood, and to distribute to each home a bright, red-covered booklet containing the Gospel of Luke, the book of Acts, and the Psalms. In the long run, Key 73 was more beneficial in our working together with other Christians in the town than it was an effective means of drawing unbelievers to the faith.

During the 1970s, cottage meetings were a new experience for Grace parishioners to simply get to know each other by name and face as well as in fellowship and service. These were voluntary gatherings once a month in different host homes for the purpose of increasing friendship and the awareness of long-standing fellowship groups at Grace Church, most notably the Women's Society and Men's Club. The cottage meetings were something of a misnomer; River Forest had no cottages. But the problem was more that too few members felt a sense of need sufficient to take one night out of each month for purposes not clearly defined. The challenge was even greater among young adults. Pairs and Spares was a well-received effort for a time, but it sputtered more than soared as the late 1970s came on. At no time later on in my Grace ministry did I ever succeed in finding effective ways to reach young adults. The church did not really have a staff for young adults and cottage meetings; thus our leadership training fell short.

Although the Women's Society was a backbone group in Grace Church throughout those years, drawing *younger* women into its service and fellowship lagged. We were not picking up on the rapidly changing culture around us in which more and more women were working outside the home. The group did organize an evening division; but because of less time and energy among working women, it was more limited than the group that had begun with a noon luncheon every first Wednesday of the month for the past seventy years. The annual sale sponsored by the Women's Society was always a day booming with activity, bringing hundreds of people to the booths and craft tables displaying the talents of Grace women. That event brought in upwards of $20,000 each year for the support of benevolence and mission ministries at home and abroad. Most important were the friendships these women formed while working together for months before the event on things they enjoyed and in which they were skilled. And they were frequently an effective channel for mutual ministry: more often than they ever realized, they ministered to me in times I needed the leaven of their hospitality and unfailing support throughout all my years at Grace.

An important connecting link to Grace's lasting and fruitful partnership with the urban mission in Chicago began in 1971. It was particularly significant because the two young missionaries with whom we became associated were both Missouri Synod pastors. Having received their first taste of inner-city ministry during their seminary vicarage in Chicago, Tom Tews and Mick Roschke were ideally suited as a team: both were young, venturesome, unafraid of new methods for new challenges, and blessed with zeal, humor, and savvy in good measure. Their turf was an area of Chicago called Uptown, whose population was composed largely of dislocated people from Appalachia, Native Americans from reservations, addicts still adrift in the wilderness of drugs and alcoholism, and refugees from places as widely scattered as Saigon, Calcutta, and Teheran. Uptown Chicago was not traditional Lutheran territory, as Tews and Roschke soon learned when they plunged into this hugely demanding urban mission. It was our good fortune that both they and their wives made Grace their church home while getting started. I admired their spunk and sought volunteers from the congregation to support their pioneering work. Two couples led the response, Walter and Maxine Christopher and Fred and Clara Schmitt, both old enough to be the young men's parents and both distinguished River Forest residents who organized food drives, clothing appeals, furniture donations, and dinners that brought Grace members and Chicago Uptown Ministry people together. When the two young pastors, who were inexperienced in real estate and mortgage matters, saw an opportunity to move from a storefront to a once-grand brownstone mansion to house the ministry but lacked the $10,000 to take it, Grace members helped put it together with nine other congregations. Two Concordia College students, Jan Neumiller and Ruth Strege, who worshiped at Grace and heard Tews and Roschke speak, volunteered their summer of 1971 as mission helpers and spent the following year in full-time service in Uptown. They stretched our Kingdom Frontiers grant of $5,000 across twelve months' cost of room and board, and regularly informed the congregation with reports of their work. During the thirty years since that Grace-Uptown hookup began, dozens of Grace members have come to know Chicago Uptown Ministry people through church dinners at both locations, food donations, clothing, and school collections, and — most important — have come to form friendships with people otherwise separated by vast social and economic barriers. It was one more channel that kept the gospel ministry central and the court battle on the sideline.

In May 1975, we joined Lutheran congregations throughout the nation in sponsoring Vietnamese refugee families through an inter-Lutheran Immigration and Refugee Service. Nguyen Thi Lieng-Hoa was the head of the first family assigned to us: she was a mother of three who arrived with her children, her mother, two teenage stepsisters, and a brother at O'Hare Airport on July 22. Grace School principal Gerald Koenig and I were the welcoming committee. My first glimpse of the family of eight coming off the plane was something I had not expected. The children were dressed in cowboy outfits and the adults in traditional Vietnamese clothing. But all broke into smiles as they spotted their misspelled names on the placards Koenig and I were carrying. We didn't know that they had all adopted Americanized first names, and in all likelihood our hopelessly misspelled versions of their Vietnamese names helped break the ice as they walked in shy bewilderment into the new world awaiting them. Among the best things the refugee family brought to us was a gift of which they had no idea. Despite our deteriorating relationship with Concordia College, Grace Church people and the college people worked together superbly in moving them immediately into an apartment provided by the college and furnished by Grace members.

Ironically, the eight Grace families that served as sponsors included people on differing sides of the synodical conflict. But when it came to rallying in support of those who had lost everything and fled for their lives from Vietnam — leaving behind a husband and father as a political prisoner somewhere in North Vietnam — nobody talked of doctrinal conflict. Everybody worked together. Robert Hamann, comptroller of West Suburban Hospital, found Lieng-Hoa an office position in which she quickly proved her competence and rose in the ranks during years of employment there. Dental and health care, school enrollment, insurance and transportation needs, tutoring in English, shopping know-how, household furnishings — right down to the details of baking pans, mop and pail, toaster, sewing machine, bedroom curtains, etc. — were all items covered by a small army of more that ninety Grace parishioners coordinated by Bill Ewald. Working side by side as volunteers were Ralph Gehrke and his arch-opponent in the synodical mess, Paul Kreiss. But in this endeavor they were partners in making the Word come alive rather than being mired in accusations about the Word. Grace joined with neighboring St. Paul's Lutheran Church in Melrose Park, an LCMS parish that was always fraternal toward us, in helping the Vietnamese family negotiate the purchase of a house.

Within two years, Lieng-Hoa's brother and wife sought relocation from Camp Pendelton, California, to be nearer their sister. Sponsoring them was also a joint Grace–St. Paul's venture, bringing to ten the number of family members sharing occupancy of the house they were paying for themselves. On two occasions I was moved deeply by how much Lieng-Hoa was giving as well as receiving. When I sent out an emergency appeal for helping victims of a killer earthquake in Guatemala, the first envelope I opened was a check for $50 from Lieng-Hoa. The other occasion came over a dozen years later when her husband, the political prisoner who had finally been freed, walked through the arrival gate at O'Hare Airport to meet his wife and his children, who now were in medical school or completing engineering degrees or holding good jobs. Their politely understated greeting of each other, almost too formal by our cultural standards, but not theirs, was a testimony to prayers answered, hopes realized, and sacrifice fulfilled as a family was reunited after war had torn them apart for twenty years.

The Sunday after the airport reunion I asked the couple to share something of the drama of their separation and reunion with the congregation. When one person, who suffered acutely from liturgical correctness, complained that their witness was too lengthy an intrusion into worship, their English too hard to understand, I wanted to crown him. But instead of that, I took comfort that all the others present that morning at Grace could experience the thrill of God's providence displayed before our eyes. Lieng-Hoa and her family were the first of a number of Vietnamese and eastern European couples and families sponsored by Grace through the years, when the shadow of litigation could not overshadow the light of faith in welcoming strangers in whom Christ's welcoming grace is hidden.

Other activities that built the nurturing spirit within the congregation by reaching out beyond us included the work of a committee formed to study Cook County Jail problems and offer our members' help. Barbara Rinnan brought well-qualified speakers to adult education sessions, and I included some of them as participants in sermons. From time to time I adapted this method to other occasions when a parishioner or guest with expertise would speak from the lectern after I had opened up a biblical text from the pulpit. Natalie Kruse kept tabs on volunteers for jail visits; Robert Carlson was our main link to organizations specializing in inmate rehabilitation.

My pace of writing pastoral letters picked up considerably throughout the decade, and few of them did not have some report, admonition, or encouragement on financial stewardship. Support for our ministry, along with membership statistics, was an obvious index of how we were faring through conflict and litigation. My concern that no faltering of nerve overtake us was hard to restrain in each pastoral letter; I really harped on meeting the costs of our ministry and mission. And I marvel at the patience and the faithfulness of the members during those years. In 1970 our budget was $297,300; by 1980 it had reached $561,162. And in 1985, the year the litigation ended, it was $764,821. By grace and with grit, the parish finished each of those years in the black, while shouldering the additional legal costs, which came to a final total of $269,609. The discipline did not hurt us. True, every one of those dollars could have been well used elsewhere. But it is also true that we had to accept the whole ordeal of litigation as a test of what we believed about the primacy of the gospel in the church and congregation. In that sense it was a ministry in spite of the collective sins of all of us, Grace and the Synod alike. After 1977 we were an independent congregation — organizationally but not ecclesiologically. We were blessed to give to benevolence and mission work at home and abroad, and by virtue of our situation maintained much closer ties with those whom we supported. The work of preaching the gospel, teaching the faith, counseling those who sought it, and the care of souls of the sick and dying remained primary.

One instance of pastoral care as the essence of my daily work in those days, undistracted by church and courtroom ruckus from the outside, stands for many more. Linda Mergen was a gentle, reserved young woman whom I had not come to know very well when she and her parents joined Grace. Then, out of the blue, cancer struck hard, and she learned within two weeks that her condition was grave, if not terminal. My pastoral visits to her West Suburban Hospital room gave me an opportunity to learn so much more about the ups and downs of her thirty years of life, and some of the downs were as heartbreaking as they were hidden. She also told me of lesser things that I never realized could loom so large in someone's fight to the finish with cancer — things such as how hard it was to ride to church on bumpy Division Street. My discomfort with irksome legal depositions and court appearances faded away when I ministered to Linda and her parents. Nothing is harder on a mother and father than watching their daughter die by inches. I recall one conversation with Fred and Louise in the hospital hallway and their question of not whether but how they should tell their daughter she was dying. But it was clear from the sadness in her eyes that Linda knew, and we knew that she knew. My calling was to turn her eyes to the cross and the sure promise of the risen Lord that she would not go alone through the valley of the shadow of death. Mercifully, her death was sooner rather than later. The courage and strength shown her by her family were a benediction on her — and on me — as I took comfort in the penumbra cast by the loyalty of love. Going with Linda through that hard journey, and with her family afterward, put things in perspective and kept them there.

One more event of major importance for the latter half of my Grace years began in 1975 with the death of Arthur Feicht, a man who had worked his way up from his start in the early Depression years as a messenger boy at the Chicago Stock Exchange to the heights of Chicago's financial world. And his wife, Bernice, was his match in the brokerage business; in fact, she was the first woman in Chicago to have a seat on the CSE. The two were becoming well established in their respective business careers when they fell in love, and they were married at Grace Church on New Year's Day, 1960. Having been baptized and raised at Grace, Bernice was a woman of strong spiritual upbringing, and we rejoiced with her when her husband joined the congregation by adult confirmation. And later we mourned with her when death took him. In my ministry to her in her time of her loss, I came to realize what an accomplished businesswoman she was in a highly competitive business that was dominated by men. Our pastor-parishioner ties deepened as our family welcomed her frequently for Sunday dinners after church during her first year alone. I knew that she wished to establish a memorial to Arthur's memory and that she was likely considering any one of the many charitable agencies he had supported. This prompted me to take the initiative for a church memorial idea; with that in mind, I invited her to join me for lunch.

She suggested the Union League Club in downtown Chicago, a venue that was beyond my range but not hers. I readily accepted, thinking that that venue might be on a par with the size of the memorial I had in mind. Knowing her style of getting straight to the point and expecting the same of others, I laid out for her the idea of a memorial fund of $50,000 that would both enhance the spiritual life of Grace Church and finance something new and uncommon in congregations anywhere — a sabbatical for its pastor. She asked how spiritual enhancement would occur and what pastoral sabbaticals were about. I answered the first part of her question by describing a program that would bring qualified people to Grace to serve as theologians-in-residence for a time; the second part would mean funding the pastor for a period of time away from the church on an approved project or program of study that would bring him back better equipped for the pastorate. She said that she would think it over.

We came together for lunch two weeks later — same venue, same table — and her answer was ready. Yes, the memorial idea appealed to her, with two stipulations. The first was practical: develop more detail about how theological leaders, teachers, or musicians would be selected. The second was even more practical: she would begin with a $5,000 grant to see whether the program could work; if it did, more funding would follow. Plus, of course, the whole memorial idea needed to be approved by the congregation. I was excited about her response and agreed with the good sense that any good idea was only an idea until proven in practice.

It was not difficult to write up the protocol for administering the fund, assigning its supervision to the elders. My role was to work with the Adult Education Committee in proposing men and women who might come in as theologians-in-residence to help lift our spiritual sights. Regarding the sabbaticals, I wrote in the customary feature of their occurrence at seven-year intervals and emphasized the main point that, by enlarging the vision of the pastor, the congregation gained.

The Feicht Memorial Fund became a part of Grace Lutheran Church in 1976, and soon a stream of gifted men and women began fulfilling its purpose. Our first participant was James Childs, a refugee from the synodical conflict who had served part-time with us for nearly a year, teaching Sunday classes and midweek seminars that focused on Christian ethics amid the realities of the daily workplace. John Gienapp came in 1978 and contributed his expertise in the connections between medical science and the church's vocation in that field. Our doctors and nurses benefited from his presence. His wife, Katie Gienapp, also participated as a theologian-in-residence with her husband; her gifts were centered in childhood education and parenting. Norman Dietz brought us his creative talents in drama: one-man plays and one-man portrayals of the Gospels that stirred many of our members to an awareness of a tradition too long lost from the Christian tradition. Paul Granlund brought to Grace his stunning sculpture and his presentations on the creativity of the Spirit in the church's calling to open itself to the gifts of artists who express their faith through their fingers and clay. Our own Walter Martin began a hallway gallery of paintings and sketches and woodcuts that he gathered from many sources, including his own fine work. Carl Schalk and Harriet Ziegenhals brought in musicians from the Chicago Symphony Orchestra and others of note to Sunday morning presentations that informed members of what lay behind the great oratorios of Handel, Bach, and others.

For years we drew on the faculty of the Lutheran School of Theology in Chicago for presentations in biblical studies and other themes. Kurt Haendel, Edgar Krentz, and Ralph Klein were among the most frequently called upon. Martin Marty's appearances always packed the Fellowship Hall for whatever subject he was asked to address, from the church in American culture to fundamentalisms in the world's major religions. Through Stephen Schmidt's contacts we were introduced to gifted theologians from Mundelein and Loyola Universities. We also invited men and women from the Divinity School of the University of Chicago, who were as interested in Grace as we were in them. The Feicht Fund gave us what we needed to support outstanding people without touching our parish budget, already strained by the extra burden of legal costs from 1977 until 1985.

My resources for keeping centered and healthy amid the pressures most certainly included my family; indeed, Beverly and our four children were second to none in this regard. Our main way of getting away was camping, which fit our budget and suited the kids. We made summertime forays to the Rockies and, when time and money were short, to Wisconsin. Through the roundabout ways of Providence, we came upon a jewel of a small, uninhabited island called Detroit Island — in Lake Michigan off the coast of Door County, Wisconsin — and bought a piece of shoreline property there. After several years of camping with the Martys, who became our Detroit Island neighbors, we were able to have a shell of a house built by carpenters from nearby Washington Island; and we finished the interior ourselves during subsequent summer vacations. Our vacation regimen called for all of the Luekings to work on the house in the morning hours and to play all afternoon in the delightfully undisturbed ambience of clean water, unspoiled beach, and well-forested land. This was truly a great place to get away. We had no electricity or phones, nor did we miss them. The change of pace was always welcome and restoring, especially when more friends and Grace parishioners bought land and added to the fun. Detroit Island continues to this day to be a haven for Beverly and me, and now for our grown children. On a piece of driftwood Beverly hand-lettered a sentiment that sums it up well: "One little corner of the earth above all others makes me smile."

A final factor — but a major one — in why conflict and litigation did not do us in during this period was my pastoral sabbatical. As our legal battle neared completion in the early 1980s, I hit upon a sabbatical idea at a time and place where I least expected it. On the Sunday after Christmas 1982, we had Andrew Miller and his parents for dinner after church. I had known Andrew from his confirmation days and had watched him develop through high school and later at Davidson College in North Carolina. He had learned about a unique and promising high school in Kenya from a Quaker friend in North Carolina, who had been headmaster of the school, which was well out into the bush on the western border. After his college graduation, Andrew had gone to this Shikhoko School and served two years as teacher and headmaster. As we sat at table listening to his enthusiasm for Africa, this thought came to me: why not go there on a sabbatical and see it firsthand — as well as other places where the church was experiencing unprecedented growth. The plot line of the sabbatical was simple: What is it like to be a Christian in this place? And the follow-up question was: How can this sabbatical experience bring back benefit to the people of Grace Lutheran Church? By the time Beverly had served dessert and coffee that Sunday, the seed of a global sabbatical journey was planted in my mind. Seven months later it would sprout, and I would be on my way.

CHAPTER 7

Ministry in Global Perspective

The world is my parish.

JOHN WESLEY

The goal of my sabbatical was to see firsthand something of the fundamental shift in global Christianity that had been developing since World War II. The direction of church mission and growth was no longer primarily westward and north, as it had been since St. Paul's missionary journeys recorded in the book of Acts. Now growth — explosive growth — was taking place primarily south of the equator in black Africa and eastward on the Pacific Rim in places such as South Korea. I wanted to learn why this seismic change had come about and what it meant for my ministry at Grace Church and beyond. For twenty years I had tried to keep up with the changing face of world mission; now an opportunity lay before me to learn from people who were directly involved in shaping those changes. More than I ever anticipated, what I experienced while abroad would put a lasting stamp on the rest of my ministry at Grace.

My first priority in preparing for the sabbatical during that late winter and spring of 1983 was to inform the congregation well beforehand of what I was about to do and why it mattered. Of course, I also needed to work out arrangements with my staff associates for the additional responsibilities they would assume. My conscience about their added duties was eased at least somewhat by the fact that in previous years I had seen to the formation of the Garbers Fund and the Bernice Johnson Fund, funds whose purposes were similar to the Feicht Fund for the pastoral sabbatical and from which teachers at Grace benefited greatly. Assistant Pastor David Schreiber assured me that he was ready for the added work he would assume. Then came the matter of arranging visits in each place on my projected sabbatical itinerary and explaining my purpose, which was summed up in a simple question: What is it like to be a Christian in your place? I drew on contacts with clergy and other friends from previous years to set up visits to congregations and schools in Europe, Israel, Kenya, India, Nepal, Thailand, Hong Kong, mainland China, South Korea, and Japan. Beverly took charge of the packing for us and our two younger children, Sarah and Joel, who were with us for the first half of the sabbatical journey from Germany through Kenya.

The first stop was a three-day visit to St. Johannes Kirche in Braunschweig, West Germany. I chose it not to learn about church growth there, but about church decline — or, better stated, how the seed of the Word was faring in hard, resistant soil. Braunschweig had been a Hitler-friendly city in the dark days of the 1930s, and it now lay in the shadow of another tyranny just beyond the Berlin Wall, a dozen miles to the east. Our hosts, Pastor Arthur Going and his wife, Nancy, arranged my visits with a cross section of the congregation, beginning with Magdalen Mollat and her husband, Hans-Juergen. They were highly committed Christians of medical mission experience in India, now among only a handful of several dozen who were active worshipers in a parish of 9,000. I picked up on their resolutely positive spirit in my first interview as they spoke of their guest pastor from India as a harbinger of this new day of two-way traffic in mission. When I asked the Mollats about what Sunday worship meant to them, they acknowledged their dismay at sitting with a few dozen others, surrounded by a sea of empty pews. Yet they were grateful for those present at worship as a sign of the faithful remnant of hearers who were doers of the Word between Sundays. As if to illustrate, the next day Magdalen took me with her to the funeral of an older man they had looked after for some time. Pastor Going conducted the service in the half-hour time slot allotted, which was preceded and followed by other pastors conducting similar half-hour funerals for those on their huge parish rosters whom they had likely not seen since a marriage, confirmation, or baptism. The experience of the morning sunk in as a telling glimpse of the dry bones of a moribund *Volkskirche* breathed to life by the Mollats, exemplars of faith active in love.

That evening the Goings gathered a group of four Germans for something Germans do very well — discuss serious issues seriously. My opening question was about what meaning the faith and the church had for their lives. The frank answer from Marion Elflaien, a nineteen-year-old dental assistant trainee, was . . . not much. Like so many of her peers, she had drifted away from her confirmation vows to grow in faith and in a way of life recognizably Christian. Her current involvement, however, as a volunteer in a congregation-sponsored kindergarten could change that. As I took notes on her comments, I thought of too many of her counterparts in too many Lutheran congregations throughout western Christendom, including Grace Church. Otto Schulze, a sixty-year-old electrical engineer, German army veteran, and former war prisoner also spoke of being confirmed in his north German village, then "leaving the church without a trace," as he put it with a sheepish grin. His story of renewal included the influence of attending a weeklong *Kirchentag,* an annual event of worship and life-related Bible studies sponsored by the Lutheran Church in Germany, a program that makes pronouncements on the death of the church in Germany premature. Ulf Mai was a twenty-year-old with one more year of required military service, a native of Braunschweig and a son of this congregation; he also spoke of spiritual drift as a postconfirmation dropout from the church. He was concerned about the treatment of South Africans who were suffering a German version of racial *apartheid* and wondered what the church here was doing about it. That sparked a pro-and-con debate, which was interrupted by the arrival of a fourth guest, Wilhelm Schaper, a musician whose description of his year in England and his experience of liturgy in the

Church of England was highlighted by a surprise: he heard humor from the pulpit and laughter in the congregation. With typical German introspection, he was probing the question that, if God is filled with grace and if the gospel is good news, why shouldn't there be times when Christians are smiling and laughing during worship?

All of these Germans spoke of the threatening presence of the Wall so close by, and all were certain that it would not come down in their lifetime. Just six years later, of course, when the Berlin Wall did come down — and Communism with it — I remembered that evening in Braunschweig and wondered what those astonishing events must have meant to those four people and millions more. How ready were they, or any of us with them, for the more pervasive threat of the idolatry of runaway capitalism and mindless consumerism? I left Braunschweig with a sense that here was a mission field of thick resistance, but that there also was a remnant of the faithful few who were seeds of a renewed church, more humbled than triumphalist, more ready to pioneer than prop up a shell of Christendom, more receptive to witnesses from afar as partners in costly discipleship. Each of these impressions would bear on my work at Grace when I returned. In addition, Arthur Going was to join us from 1984 to 1986 as an assistant pastor on our staff.

We drove our rental car from Braunschweig westward for a brief visit with my relatives an hour west of Hanover, then south through Switzerland and Austria, and across the Danube into Czechoslovakia. The border crossing was a pain: papers to fill out, all the luggage to haul out, and the requirement to pay 44 of our filthy capitalist dollars for every day we were in the socialist paradise. Beverly's Slovak language fluency helped, and we finally finished the red tape and drove on past border guards (tripled since our 1976 crossing) stationed in guard towers with machine guns pointed our way, and over a mile of barbed-wire barriers to keep the bodies and souls of human beings in and people like us out.

The oppressive pall hanging over the border crossing gave way to the heart-warming, waist-expanding hospitality of Beverly's cousins in Bratislava, this capital city of a half million. I parked our rental Ford in the long line of cars waiting to get gas while Beverly searched for something not easy to find, a public telephone with a phone book. Then a lovely thing happened, something that puts a human face on the blurred anonymity of a strange place. The woman in charge of a coffee stand in the station helped Beverly find her cousins' number and make the call, and then insisted on getting into her small, smoke-spouting Skoda to lead us directly to the address we would otherwise have taken hours to find — if at all. There were no street signs in Bratislava: they had been removed in 1968 to confuse the Russians arriving in tanks. Our nameless friend's helpfulness was not memorable to anyone except us that day, but it reminded me of the importance of the blessing of spontaneous hospitality whenever and wherever one finds it.

As it turned out, we had been no more than five minutes away from cousin Darina Matej and her husband, Matus, whom we had met seven years earlier. She was a lawyer who by sheer grit had held onto a government position responsible for the legal side of placing abused and orphaned children in adoptive homes. As a fiercely resolute Christian, she somehow managed to find families where children could get care for their souls as well as their bodies, for which she was rewarded with no end of grief from her boss, a Party *apparatchik.* She greeted us with Slavic warmth and emotion — hugs, laughter, tears, and a torrent of words and gesticulations to the effect that "sheer chaos, total anarchy, still prevail," but that we should sit down for a cup of coffee anyway. She could attend church now, in contrast to earlier times when her government job was threatened by being seen in public worship. Now, however, she was distressed by too many lukewarm clergy and compromised Christians. The next evening we drove the Matejs to downtown Bratislava, where we entered a commercial building identified as a place of worship by a small, door-panel sign indicating that the "Church of the Brethren" met there.

We entered and found ourselves in a large space that had been gutted entirely and redone by church members; they had transformed it into a sanctuary highlighted by the beauty of natural wood crafted with Slovakian excellence. Some 200 people were present. The pastor was out of town, so a lay leader led the hymns, accompanied by a pianist in a military uniform. At the time for intercessory prayers, each one stood to speak petitions for others (Beverly translated for me) as well as for the church and nation now in its forty-third year under heavy-handed Communism. Following each prayer, the congregation responded with a firm "Amen." Then the worship leader turned to me with a look that said he wanted me to say something. I spoke, but not before taking a moment to look into the many faces, wanting to express with my silence my respect for them and humility in their presence. I brought greetings from Grace Church, spoke of the love of Christ that makes us one, and added a brief sketch of my sabbatical journey ahead. The response to the latter was palpably emotional, as people leaned forward to hear every word Beverly translated, straining to imagine what it would mean — not to cross an ocean, but just to cross the Danube and breathe the air of freedom. One man told me afterward of how he often climbed the steep palisades overlooking the Danube and gazed across into Austria, then returned to his house reassured that freedom was still visible over there. Little did I know that evening that sixteen years later I would return to Bratislava as an emeritus pastoral ambassador from Grace Church to teach in their Lutheran seminary.

We managed a short trip three hours north to one of the most beautiful valleys I have seen anywhere. Karlova, the birthplace of Beverly's father, and nearby Blatnice, where he was baptized, were home to other relatives. Their parting gift to us after a delightful visit was a bottle of homemade *slivovice,* with the insistence that we take a sip each morning. It paid off. We had not a single day of stomach upset throughout the journey. No bug could possibly survive the cleansing wallop this plum brandy carried.

Arriving by air in Tel Aviv revived my memory of Israeli airport security, surely the tightest in the world because of the terrorism that dominates so much of life in the Holy Land. Our week there was centered in Jerusalem, where my first contact was Ja'akov Ariel, an Israeli doctoral student at the University of Chicago under Martin Marty (who had given me his name). He answered my opening question, "Are Israelis bitter?" with an immediate "Yes, and many have a right to be." To my surprise, however, he was speaking for the 80,000 Arabs who are Israeli

citizens but relegated to second-class status through government poli-
cies that alternatively benefit or inflame them, compounded by the injustice of confiscating their land for new Israeli settlements. My host
was not an incendiary person but an intelligent, caring man actively engaged in strengthening Israel by ensuring Palestinian rights. Listening
to him made me wonder how differently Middle East history would
read if his view, and its counterpart on the West Bank, would have prevailed.

My contacts with Palestinian Christians were arranged by Al and
Lois Glock, Grace Church parishioners who had moved to the West
Bank for biblical archaeological research and teaching at Bir Zeit University. Al was not amused by visitors who came through and heard only
the Israeli side of the complex story; during my two previous visits to the
Holy Land, he had taken pains to tell me what I didn't know about Palestinian Christians, whom I would now have the privilege of meeting.
Vohan Melikian received me in his tiny stamp-collector shop less than a
hundred yards from the Church of the Holy Sepulcher in the Old City of
Jerusalem. His Armenian background made him a member of a minority group of Arab peoples: his father had fled Turkey and settled in Jerusalem, where he raised his family on land he owned and passed on to his
children. Vohan was the second of three sons, born in Jerusalem and educated during a time when Palestinian and Jewish boys could be friends
and later have amicable business relationships. That changed dramati-
cally when the Israeli government took his land, his house, and his business property. Then his wife died, leaving him with his four daughters
to raise.

"Are you bitter?" I asked. He answered with a sigh that bitterness
was a luxury he could not afford, and then quoted the Lord's Prayer petition "forgive us our trespasses as we forgive those who trespass
against us" as a case-closed end of that subject. He had to stay strong for
his daughters, two of whom were studying abroad.

"Would you emigrate if you could?" I asked in response to his concern about the brain drain of gifted Palestinian youth leaving the country. His answer was yes, "to anyplace warm"; but really his answer was
no, because his ninety-three-year-old mother "would not let her little

boy out of her sight." The next morning I sat with him and his youngest daughter in Hope Lutheran Church in Ramallah, twenty-five minutes north of Jerusalem. He spoke of his satisfaction in helping start up this congregation as a charter member in 1951, as well as his pride in the adjoining school building for 500 children, which had been built with help from Lutherans in Sweden. The majority of the 250 parishioners were Arabs who had been educated in Lutheran schools in Ramla, Jaffa, and other coastal areas. His appreciation of Lutheran schools as a primary means of mission outreach was matched by my comment that it was the same at our Grace School.

Vohan's two major concerns for the future were the emigration of gifted Palestinian youth, caused in part by the refusal of major Arab nations to receive Palestinian teachers, engineers, other professionals, and business leaders — who are more numerous in proportion to their population than in any other nation in the Arab world. His other concern was the diminution in personal contacts of any depth between Jews and Arabs, which was creating a vacuum all too ready to be filled by terrorist groups on the West Bank. Melikian showed me enough in several meetings to make me regard him as a rarity among West Bank Palestinians, much as Ja'akov Ariel was among Israelis. Unfortunately, the shrinking number of people like them on both sides has meant fateful consequences in the escalating violence that has dominated the bloody years since 1987.

We spent our final day in Israel with Albert and Lois Glock in their hospitable home, and it was a good opportunity for us to share our impressions of the visits with Palestinian Christians. Both Al and Lois spoke of their hopes and fears for what lay ahead. But none of us realized that day that the lethal violence of the region would strike their household within a decade. Al Glock was shot dead in the doorway of a colleague's house in 1991 by an assassin who has yet to be found. I won't forget taking the news to his son, Jeff, a teacher at Grace School, and conducting the memorial service for Al, our first Grace Church martyr. That shock focused my memory on the conversations with West Bank Christians, real people with real struggles amid the chaotic, zigzag course of rock-throwing and missiles, land grabs and suicide bombings, roadblocks and terrorist reprisals, which make all of us want to turn away and hear no more. On the West Bank and in Israel they cannot turn away.

The five weeks we spent in Kenya provided us with the longest, most sustained look at church life where it was growing exponentially as in few other places in the world. In 1900 there were 5,000 Christians in this country of 2.9 million — .02 percent of the population. As a massive influx of Catholic and Protestant missionaries arrived after 1900, and reached remote tribes by roads and railways unreachable before that, the blessing on their labors has come through in these astonishing statistics: by 1948, 30 percent of the population was Christian, with the numbers of converts doubling, sometimes tripling, year by year thereafter. By 1962 it had reached 54 percent, and by 1970, 63 percent. By 1983, the year of my visit, there were an estimated 11,450,000 Christians in Kenya, or 73 percent of its 15.7 million population. But there were also 269 registered denominations and sects among the Christians, indicating the major problem of internal disunity that came with the phenomenal external growth. These were facts that brought me to Kenya with hopes of meeting people who would put flesh on the bare bones of the numbers.

After a few days of orientation in Nairobi, we boarded a bus at 5:30 a.m. for the ten-hour journey of two hundred miles westward. It was already crowded with men heading off to nearby towns, anxious mothers keeping track of sleepy youngsters and crying babies, suitcases, boxes, furniture, squawking chickens, and one goat. I wanted to take the day bus instead of the faster night train in order to see the Great Rift Valley and everything else along this route that passed by tea plantations and coffee farms, occasional herds of giraffes, dairy cattle, and village after village of huts with grass-thatched roofs that dot the landscape. The bus, not the latest in ground transportation, stopped often for passengers to get on and off, many of whom did a double take when they saw us. In front of us sat a mother and her four-year-old son, the only ones who were with us for the trip all the way to Kisumu, on the northeast shore of Lake Victoria. From there we negotiated the last twenty miles to our destination via a *matatu,* a pickup truck with benches for passengers on either side; a dozen or more in addition to us were squeezed onto that *matatu* for the forty-five minute trip.

We finally disembarked at "the first tall tree after crossing the bridge over the Yala River," as our host Andrew Miller had described the bus stop; but when we saw nothing of Andrew, who had missed our telegram, we stood for a while by the roadside looking lost. Presently, a tall Kenyan noticed our plight and called out to a group of women to carry our four sizable suitcases. Off we went on the two-mile foot trek with each woman bearing a fifty-pound suitcase on her head. We wound along a red-dirt path through small garden plots, alongside more grass-roofed huts, down through a steep gorge and up the opposite side that opened onto a beautiful meadow with a panoramic view for miles around. We reached our host's house an hour before he returned, unloaded our bags, and stood in a circle in the kitchen with hands clasped as each woman prayed a fervent prayer of thanksgiving for our safe arrival and hope for our prosperous stay in this place. Their thanks for my payment came with a firm handshake, broad smiles, and a torrent of words in their tribal Kiluhya language, matched by my enthusiastic compliments for African women who can carry such loads on their heads — at a brisk pace, with arrow-straight posture, at an elevation of 5,000 feet, without being winded. Andrew Miller arrived, supper was prepared, the sun went down, and I went to sleep with the vivid awareness that the Third World was no longer an abstraction. This was Africa — the real Africa.

The month in western Kenya was a rich experience for Sarah and Joel, who walked daily to the *harambe* (Swahili for "let's pull together") school where Andrew Miller was the headmaster. They were careful not to wander off the narrow path into places where Black Mamba snakes, whose venom can kill in four minutes, were sometimes seen. They were the two white children among the 500 students of middle- and high-school age, all of whom were trilingual. Every day Beverly walked the mile and a half — across the Equator from the Southern to the Northern Hemisphere — to an outdoor market, making sure to return before the mid-afternoon shower that fell with clocklike regularity at that time of year. The buckets under the downspouts caught the rainwater for our daily supply of safe drinking water.

Among the dozens of people I interviewed, two were especially representative of what I had come to study. Isaac Lidonde was a native of the village of Shikokho, the local boy who had made good. He was a man in his mid-fifties, the son of a strong Christian family, who was not able to start school before age ten because British colonial rule forbade it. His training under Friends missionary educators awakened an awareness of his exceptional intellectual and spiritual capacities. He wanted to become a doctor, but at that time British colonial law also ruled that out, so he settled for medical technology and graduated from the University College in Nairobi. He married Mary, a grace-filled woman, who in later years stayed home in Kenya with their young family during the year Isaac spent in graduate study in hematology in Birmingham, England. Isaac spoke of how he reshaped African traditions by his Quaker heritage, including this view: "I told them we had to speak and that no African could sit in silence for an hour." There was an intensity about the man that grew as he reflected on what it means to be a Christian in his time and place. He summarized it in three themes: first, Kenyan Christians need Kenyan leadership, of course, but he regretted the abrupt departure of foreign missionaries after 1963. Christianity is by its very nature transnational, and gifted Christians from outside Kenya were still needed for the church to be at its best. Second, it has proven a romantic fallacy to assume that Kenyan Christians could move into full leadership positions overnight; too few were thoroughly trained in sound theology and church leadership. His plea that some missionaries return, not as the bosses but as servant leaders committed to training for leadership, was part of his realism about the consequences of petty jealousies, power struggles, and plain incompetence in the church. Third, he saw a need for the church to produce more laity of moral character who could leaven the nation by practicing honesty and responsibility in their calling as national leaders. He saw the rapidly emerging independent nations of Africa as desperately in need of such laity and cited the current president of Kenya, Daniel Moi, as a template for the youth of the nation, who comprised 60 percent of the population. After listening to him, I came away convinced that Lidonde himself, more than President Moi, is the template for leadership needed in the nation and church. It is regrettable that

Moi's leadership performance in recent years has not held up as well as Isaac Lidonde's record of inspired service in church and nation.

Francis Alulu is a lay catechist in the Catholic parish near Andrew Miller's house. He gave me generous amounts of his limited time for interviews on the daily work of these laity, who bear a major share of the pastoral side of church life in and beyond Kenya. He is full-time in ministry, married, and the father of seven children. He was formerly an engineer trained in engine maintenance, but his gifts for teaching the Bible caught the attention of his priest, and he took the two-year course for catechists and was assigned to Shitoli parish. Before beginning our conversation in his small office room of the church, he read Ephesians 3:12-20 and prayed that God would bring good from our words — a prayer offered in the flowing spontaneity characteristic of African spirituality. Then he presented a well-organized discourse on the range of his duties.

The parish numbers 11,000 souls and is linked with three others to form a regional membership of 30,000 baptized Catholics. No full-time priest serves Shitoli; one comes to celebrate Mass each Sunday after serving the other two parishes. Otherwise, all daily responsibilities are in Alulu's hands: adult catechesis at 8 a.m. each weekday morning for the sixty who attend; visitation by foot to the sick within a six- to seven-mile radius; reconciling people caught up in feuds, property disputes, and dowry hassles; and regular participation in the fourteen organizational units that bring all members together at intervals for prayer, Scripture, discussion of family and work problems, consoling the bereaved, and organizing food drives for starving Catholics and non-Catholics alike (this last being especially crucial in the spring before crops mature). He prepares couples for marriage through retreats and day-long sessions on practical aspects of marriage, presides at funerals (I attended one that began at 10:00 and ended at 2:00), instructs children in doctrine and liturgy each Saturday from 8 a.m. until 1:00 p.m., trains lectors for the Mass, conducts penitential services for those needing counsel, and participates in the Sunday Mass as hymn leader and assistant in the Eucharist, often following up the priest's homily with applications for the parish problems he knows best. The average attendance at Sunday Mass is 700, which is all the open-sided building can accommodate. Alulu's modest income comes from contributions of money, vegetables, maize, and chickens — all brought forward with the Eucharistic bread and wine. The last Sunday that we attended Mass, Francis sent us off with prayer and well-wishing, plus a live chicken which he placed in Joel's arms, a first for him and a moment none of us will forget.

Why is the church growing at such an unprecedented rate in Kenya and throughout black Africa? Because, like the wind, the Holy Spirit blows where it wills, and no one can program the mystery of its timing nor the places of its choosing. Because the poor in spirit are blessedly open to the kingdom of heaven. Because belonging to Christ means belonging to the people whom he gathers. Because the seed of the gospel grows better in a culture of sharing rather than competing. Because there is a time for everything, including this time when the labors of four centuries of Christian mission in Kenya has brought results no one could have imagined during the long decades of dormancy.

How is it growing? Through laity like Lidonde and Alulu and countless others who take on immense loads of daily work and carry it, like the four women carrying our suitcases on their heads, with singing and the straight-arrow posture of commitment. My five weeks in Kenya have been followed by lively, ongoing ties between Grace Church and the Christians there. We have shared with them our blessings in support for schools, students, plus two Grace parishioners who have taught at Shikokho School. High on the list of their gifts to us is ongoing contact with the astonishing activity of the Spirit of God among them and the infusion of energy their zeal provides me whenever I think I am overworked.

I was unprepared for India. The taxi ride from the Bombay airport into the city was more than a way to get from one point to another; it was a numbing exposure to thousands of humans living in cardboard- or canvas-covered shacks several yards off the road, where disease is king, squalor its kingdom, and misery its way of life. From the poverty of Indian villages people have come by the millions to Bombay and other cities — seeking a better life and finding it worse. More than any other place in the world I had seen, India's poverty was overpowering. It took me days to adjust enough to be about what I was there for.

India, of course, is not endless slums and starvation. The hospitality, intelligence, and commitment of Indian Christians whom I met at the southern tip of the country introduced me to a microcosm of church life among the 27 million Indian Christians, 4 percent of the population. From among the many Indian clergy and laity I met, two are like bookends in their contrasting answers to my question of what the Christian life means in their time and place.

For Martha Seralvialai it meant nothing less than survival. She is a leper, one among the 3.3 million Indians who suffer from this disease. She was born into an upper-caste Hindu family, attended school through the sixth grade, became a bride at thirteen through an arranged marriage, and was on her way to her future in the traditional life of a South India woman. Ten years later she felt a numbness in her feet and learned that the dreaded onset of leprosy was irreversible. Her son left the family immediately to be raised by relatives, and she has not seen him since. Her husband moved away after leaving her alone in a two-room hut, then sold the other half to inhospitable people and gave the sale money to his sister. Her plight became known to Virginia Meinzen, wife of thirty-five-year missionary veteran Luther Meinzen, who befriended Martha. Sustained in body and soul by local Christians, Martha has come to the faith and, despite her crippled condition, visits fellow lepers at a nearby hospital, taking Christian literature and her own witness to those shunned as lepers have been shunned for ages. Virginia Meinzen introduced me to her and asked permission to tell me her story. As Virginia unfolded its drama, Martha began to weep silently. When asked if there was some new problem she answered, "No, these are tears of joy, because Jesus won't abandon me nor will you, my Christian sister."

P. A. Varkey is a business executive who has retired after a distinguished career with one of India's largest tea companies. This tall, lithe, immaculately groomed man of 72 received me for morning tea in his handsome residence, where he gave me an abbreviated version of his life story. He then took me by car to a bungalow in which 100 children were gathered, from six to sixteen years in age. The building and program of Christian education going on inside were Varkey's memorial to his late wife. He employed ten teachers to guide the children in a regular school curriculum, enriched by Scripture stories, prayer, dancing, and songs they were now singing with gusto — all the while glancing our way to see if we were singing along. Varkey explained that most of the children are from non-Christian homes but come at the invitation of neighboring Christian families and stay because of the superior educational program and the ambience of brightly colored floormats and mural-covered walls.

Following that visit, Varkey picked up another layman and an Orthodox priest to join us in several days of nonstop visits to pastors, congregations, schools, and a medical clinic. He steered through streets jammed with vendors, cows, food stands, children, shops, shoppers — sounding his car horn incessantly all the way. Above the clatter of it all, we carried on a surprisingly productive conversation about his assessment of things in the church. He named greed and factionalism as the two main enemies from within. His hope for the church centered in a laity strong enough in faith to break such barriers as the rigid protocol that separated management from labor, a problem he knew personally from his working years. He described times of kneeling in prayer out in tea fields when drought struck, which his crusty British boss frowned on but said nothing more about when the rains came. Varkey told such stories to the people of Grace Church several years later when he visited us and spoke to the congregation in a Sunday service and to the children in a Sunday school assembly where he was as thoroughly at home with our kids as he was back home in his bungalow school.

Nepal — "the hidden kingdom" — was closed to Christians and to most of the world, in fact, until 1951. This was but the first of many things I learned from a ruddy-cheeked, white-haired Jesuit priest, Marshal Moran. He was the first resident Christian missionary ever in this kingdom of 15 million people set within fabled high mountain scenery, with a history rich in Hindu religion and culture. My host and seminary classmate, medical missionary Richard Matern, took me to the boys school forty-five minutes outside Katmandu, which Fr. Moran had founded in 1951. After I learned that his brother ran an auto repair shop five minutes south of Grace Church, a coincidence we celebrated with a glass of sherry, Moran launched into a mini-lecture on the Christian story in the land. He was not the first missionary; Indian Christians had come into Nepal for years as underground missionaries, but their work left no historical tracks. Moran was allowed entry because of his credentials as an educator, and after buying the former residence and grounds of the prime minister for his campus, he made the school an institution of such excellence that it attracted children of the royal family. Also, his personal ties to Gandhi and Nehru during his twenty-one years as a missionary in India added prestige to his name. Thus a way opened for him in 1951 to become registered and officially recognized as the first resident Christian, and his school was accepted as such.

I had known and admired Richard Matern from our days together at Concordia Seminary. With a zest for mission that propelled him through seminary, through medical school, through medical mission service among Navajo Indians in Arizona, and through work as a surgeon in Vietnamese civilian hospitals, he had come to Nepal in the late 1970s. He began his medical mission service in Katmandu and outlying Himalayan villages, often performing cleft pallet surgeries by candlelight in one-room houses. He hosted us in his home, which also served as a clinic for patients who lined up at dawn for the only medical service available to them. The quintessential doctor, Matern came through at a petrol stand one noon hour when we were fueling up his Vespa motor scooter. A young Nepali approached him for a handout. Dick spoke to him in acceptable Nepali, asking him to pull up his shirt for a look at the skin on his stomach and back. As the somewhat befuddled young man complied, Matern put his hands gently on either side of the man's temples and looking closely at the skin condition on and under his eyelids. As the gas tank was about to run over, Matern told the man he had leprosy and where medical help could be found. It was but one of numerous moments of hands-on care I witnessed while making rounds with Matern to clinics, hospitals, drug centers, house churches, and schools. The overall impact was more inspiring than the massive grandeur of the Himalayas, which formed a suitable backdrop for work among some of God's most indomitable and beleaguered children on earth.

In the northeast corner of Thailand, located a few miles from the Thai-Laotian border, ten thousand refugees live in a place I wanted to visit. They are the Hmong people of Laos, one segment of over a million Southeast Asian refugees who fled Vietnam, Cambodia, and Laos as victims of war, tribal rivalries, Communist opportunism, capitalist graft, and overall human savagery. The million who made it to Nam Yao, one of thirteen refugee camps maintained by the United Nations, survived the more hidden holocaust that took the lives of four million in the killing fields of Southeast Asia. Before visiting them, I knew little of their plight; their misery was kept at a distance by their strange-sounding names and their even lesser-known political, cultural, and religious history.

The lay leader of the congregation of several hundred Christians in the camp was Doong Lu Shoong; he, his wife, and his four sons were in their eighth year as Hmong refugees from Laos. Shoong's wife, Blia, was dressed in the multi-colored, floor-length garment that partly covered her bare feet. Their house was one large room with partitions for sleeping, a kitchen, and a main living area. The handmade furniture was spare, the clay floor immaculate with straw mat rugs placed here and there. The couple blended reserve with friendliness as they spoke with me through an interpreter. Neither one of them had much chance for schooling during the chaotic 1960s; both were Christians who spoke of their faith as the anchor that held their lives together through almost constant disruption. At Nam Yao, Doong worked in the bakery of the camp, which he showed me with pride in the delicious bread from ovens fired by hand-powered bellows. His wife joined in the main work of women of the camp, intricate needlework that produced designs for varied uses — all at the risk of ruining their eyes because of inadequate lighting. Doong was well grounded in Scripture and devoted what time he had to leading worship, teaching and preaching, visiting members in the camp who were suffering ennui, the main malady of refugee camp life. He quoted a passage from St. Paul that summed up the status quo of his life and ministry: "A

145

wide door for effective work has been opened to me, and there are many adversaries" (1 Cor. 16:9).

My host for this visit was Don Ruleson, an American missionary who had spent 1945 through 1951 in China with the China Inland Mission. When the Communists expelled all Christian missionaries, he and his wife, Kathy, continued CIM work in northern Thailand until 1965, when sickness forced his return to the United States. He returned to Thailand when he recovered and signed on for refugee work among the Hmong in Thailand. He was fluent in twelve languages and dialects of the peoples he had served, and, though he was quiet and unassuming in manner, he was all attention when a Laotian needed his help, counsel, or prayer. He spent as much time with non-Christians as Christians in the camp, and he kept no statistics on conversions as the measure of his vocation. What did Christianity mean to him where he was? It meant the ministry of presence, ranging from helping locate overseas relatives for refugees to negotiating with buyers of Hmong crafts to witnessing to God's way of dealing with tragedy in life to performing weddings and burying the dead. We were overnight guests in the Ruleson stilt house in Pua, the closest town to the refugee camp. Their Toyota pickup was parked in a ground-level shelter surrounded by sturdy beams of native teakwood that served as stilts supporting the living quarters on the second floor level. Sitting at their breakfast table the next morning, I could reach outside a large open window and take fruit from the trees.

That evening Andy Bishop joined us from Bangkok on his regular rounds as director of the refugee assistance program of the Christian and Missionary Alliance, a relatively small denomination based in America that has placed a thousand missionaries in over forty-eight countries of the world. His response to the meaning of faith in his life was his vocation of Christian presence, with emergency help for the many troubled spots of the world where he had served. Because of his instant likeability, an almost boyishness in his offhand manner of describing ministry in place after place of hunger, disease, violence, and homelessness, I had to think that those depressed by the blight of refugee living could not help catching some glimmer of hope from this man of understated grace under pressure. Doong Lu Shoong and Blia, Don and Kathy Ruleson, and Andy Bishop were exemplars of refugee ministries that shed new light on the old truth that, while we have no continuing city here, the present one is filled with refugees whose plight we may not ignore.

The approach to the landing at Hong Kong's (old) airport in downtown Kowloon made it the most spectacular, if not hair-raising, descent anywhere. The Crown Colony offered a patchwork of stunning contrasts of steep hills covered with greenery, rising up sharply from rows of brilliant white stone skyscrapers, fronted by the emerald waters of the South China Sea. After days in Nepal and a remote Thai refugee camp, the electric atmosphere of the city that never sleeps, this Mecca of capitalism and duty-free paradise for shoppers, had a beckoning magnetism that for all its glitter could not entirely obscure the shadow of the 1997 Question: What will happen when the Republic of China takes over? That was the unspoken, and sometimes much-spoken, backdrop to my sabbatical question of how the good news of the gospel was faring amidst nervous prosperity.

James Hu, pastor of True Light Lutheran Church, had thoughtful responses to that inquiry as we sat together in a front pew of a sanctuary that seats 800. He began by pointing to the greenery of living plants around the altar as welcome reminders of God's creation amid so much steel and stone in the man-made city. He explained the function of the glassed-in booth off to the side with equipment for translating into other languages the Cantonese language used in worship. The architecture featured not a Gothic nave but a rounded style that brought people closer to each other and made better use of land in a city of stratospheric real-estate costs. The six-story building next door was a beehive of church offices serving various ministries and church-related groups. Just beyond stood the Lutheran High School, a flagship among Lutheran schools anywhere in the world. Pastor Hu had been born into a Christian family in Hunan Province and, like so many young Chinese, had left home for relatives in the south during the 1930s to escape the ravages of Japanese occupation. Following World War II, he came with his wife and family to Hong Kong, where he studied for the Lutheran ministry.

The flood of refugees from the mainland in the Communist take-over in 1949 had not only sharply increased the population but had also raised the ratio of Christians in Hong Kong from 2 percent to 18 percent by 1983. The congregation now had a thousand members, 30 percent of whom were under thirty, with three youth groups meeting each week that averaged eighty per group. Such numbers impressed me; at Grace Church we had experienced nothing close to it. The 1997 Question had something to do with it; Hu was convinced that it had created an even stronger undertow of uncertainty among youth and thus their need for belonging in a community with a message that God was sufficient for 1997 and after. Most of his parishioners did not have the luxury of a choice to leave Hong Kong for Australia or North America, nor did he consider it an option for himself and family. He spoke of Luther's theme of the theology of the cross — faith that clings to the hidden power of the crucified Lord — as increasingly relevant for ministry to those who cannot escape but must be inwardly strong for whatever comes.

Pastor Hu singled out preaching as the most potent means he had for equipping people to hold steady amid the unsettling realities of the present. The proclamation of Christ crucified and risen had proved sufficient in all his years before, personally and pastorally; he had no reason to think the future would be otherwise. Every generation, he noted, was challenged to believe the Word amid uncertainty; what made Hong Kong unique was a calendar date hanging visibly on its horizon. Hu joined with other Christian leaders in Hong Kong in writing a declaration of Christian affirmation, intended as a tool to help anchor believers, Protestant and Catholic alike, in faith and life in Hong Kong as well as strengthen ties with Christians in the People's Republic of China. He showed it to me as a timely expression of his own answer to what Christianity meant for this time and place.

Beverly and I enjoyed an evening with Philip Shen, head of the department of religion at the Chinese University of Hong Kong. He was still the man of tasteful reserve, spiritual warmth, and intellectual acumen whom I remembered well from twenty-five years before when we were fellow doctoral students under Jaroslav Pelikan at the University of Chicago. It was an evening of conversation on a wide range of topics, made all the more memorable by the lights of Hong Kong visible in the distance. The time with Shen also prepared me better than anything else for the coming days in mainland China. Another experience that made the Hong Kong–Grace Church connection real was the hospitality of Jan and Greg Westrick. Jan was a teacher at the Hong Kong Lutheran High School and had grown up in Grace congregation and school, the daughter of Carl and Noel Schalk of our parish. And one final item from my Hong Kong notebook: Beverly shopped with the best of the Hong Kong melee and came up with a dining room set to celebrate our twenty-fifth wedding anniversary gift to each other — at Hong Kong prices.

How could I even begin to comprehend what my sabbatical question would mean in the People's Republic of China, home to one out of every four humans on earth, and — to quote Winston Churchill's aphorism — "a riddle wrapped in a mystery inside an enigma"? I did not land in Shanghai with illusions of grasping China in ten days; but neither did I think our arrangement of going without hotel reservations anywhere on our itinerary would work as easily as it did. My extraordinarily good fortune of solid interviews with government-recognized congregations, underground church people, and the vice-president of the Nanjing Theological Seminary — all without previous appointment — was no small miracle. Two people, both residents of Souzhou but otherwise worlds apart, drew together the many facets of my China experience into a strand of impressions as lasting as any of the sabbatical journey.

Liu Guh Liang (the family name comes first) was a twenty-one-year-old tour guide of the China Travel Service, a.k.a. the arm of the Communist party, who intended to get maximum U.S. dollars from tourists while confining foreign tourists to a minimum of politically approved sites. I booked him for two days in Souzhou through the hotel where we negotiated a room. He appeared at 8 a.m. on the morning we had arranged, greeting us in good English and a clue to his sense of humor with his follow-up comment: "I'm working on a New Jersey accent." We were in his care for the next hours of visiting places that helped us understand why Souzhou is called the Venice of the Orient. At a park late in the afternoon, however, he surprised me by asking if we had a cross or a book that would help him understand the Bible. I suspected that the question was a trap, but it turned out he was sincere. He explained that a Bible given him by his uncle, a Christian, made no sense. Could I help him? That evening in our hotel room, as Beverly stitched together a cloth cross, I wrote a two-page overview of the salvation history of the Bible, and we gave them to him the next day. He knew that I was a Christian pastor; the time seemed right for him to open up about basic life questions, which he summed up as smoking too much while searching for some clue to a purpose in life.

We talked about such things on what was to be his last day with us. But he offered to get our train tickets back to Shanghai and suggested that he bring them to our hotel the first thing the next morning. Exactly as promised, he phoned us from the lobby, raced up the back stairs to our seventh-floor room (to avoid the security people posted at key desks outside every elevator stop and alongside the main stairway), hurried to our room door, handed me the tickets, and — all out of breath — asked, "Would you get on your knees with me and pray to God that my life might amount to something?" I did so in a prayer that lasted the thirty seconds he could risk, paid him, hugged him, and he was gone. He put himself in no small jeopardy by doing what he did. I have continued to trust that God honored that risk and is answering the prayer Liu Guh Liang requested.

We met Margaret Chang quite by accident while waiting in the Protestant Church in Souzhou, an hour before the service began. She was among the worshipers filing in well before the service in order to sing hymns and visit, as we learned. She spotted us in a waiting room, introduced herself in perfect English, and took over. The Chinese tour guide, sullen because we had insisted on going to church, was at least fifty years her junior and thus had no choice. Age still matters in China, and Margaret gracefully upstaged the tour guide with commentary on everything during the two-hour service, including the hour-long sermon, in a church packed to the doorways with 800 people. In the few minutes we had outside the church afterward, I invited Margaret to join us for lunch. She knew that that was impossible, and she warned me to say nothing to the guide about her request for my card, which I gave her with the request that she write me. She did. We invited her to come to Grace Church for a month visit as one who would tell stories of faith and life during the best and the worst of times in China. She had her visa and the air tickets we sent her when we received word from her son of her sudden illness and death in the spring of 1984. We must now wait for the reunion. It will surely come.

South Korea was the other stop on my sabbatical journey that was comparable to Kenya in the quantum leap of Christian growth. In 1900, .5 percent of the Korean population was Christian. By 1970, in South Korea it was 15 percent; 21 percent in 1975; and by 1983 it had reached 27 percent. Korean Christians themselves offered the best guide to understanding this phenomenon, exemplified by the first person I met, Pastor Hae Chul Kim, the dean of Lutheran clergy in Seoul and dean of Luther Seminary. I followed him through a typical Sunday: leading worship and preaching at the 11 a.m. service; a traditional meal of *kimchi;* then an hour meeting with the church council, then an unexpected treat — an hour with Brother Johann Danell of the Taizé Community in France, while Pastor Kim led a Bible study; and at 3:00 a youth service held jointly with another congregation, which ended at 4:30. I presume Pastor Kim took the rest of the day off.

But our schedule continued full pace that Sunday as Dr. Maynard Dorow, a friend of mine from seminary days, took us downtown to the world's largest congregation. The Central Full Gospel Church claims 270,000 members and is led by Pastor Yonggi Cho. "Big" is the operative word for everything there: the mammoth 25,000-seat sanctuary, the attendance of 150,000 at the five Sunday services, 10,000 members joining each month, a choir of 70, well-trained ushers to move crowds in and out, headphones offering translations into numerous languages, and so forth. It was far too much to digest in the hour that we attended. I gained more in our next visit, which was to a smaller (!) church of 60,000, where I interviewed Rev. Chang Ok Oh, one of the pastoral staff of twenty-one at the Young Nak Presbyterian Church. The membership is divided into nineteen parishes, each served by a full-time pastor. These in turn are subdivided into 1,362 districts, which enable a system of regular and purposeful mutual ministry among the 17,000 households. The Korean talent for passion in commitment and organization down to the last detail came through impressively. Rev. Oh answered my questions forthrightly, beginning with what makes Young Nak congregation flourish: "God the Holy Spirit!" he fairly shouted as he pointed upward. Then he went on to name other factors: the modest lifestyle of the members, sound in biblical belief and generous in tithing money, time, and talent. Each morning a prayer group gathers at dawn to pray for the church and world that day. Nonstop evangelism was centered in personal outreach through family, neighborhood, and work places. This congregation sent missionaries and money to fledgling churches in Thailand, Guam, Indonesia, Pakistan, and the Philippines. A special evangelism outreach went to military personnel, hospitals, and police stations. Seven adult choirs sing during the seven services on Sunday, and there is no difficulty in finding Koreans who want to sing and sing very well. The approximately 4,000 teens and college members are served by 300 trained youth leaders; the Sunday school teaching staff of 500 serves 2,000 children each Sunday.

The picture was the same in our rounds to other congregations and clergy, differing only in scale but similar in zeal. All of this is astounding, and it is not easy to explain — nor should we be overly quick to criticize the prominence of statistics. While nearly numbed by the numbers, I kept asking myself if criticism made sense from outsiders like me, and whether I needed to first earn the right to offer criticism through long years of firsthand presence and seasoned thought in understanding the background of this massive thrust of the Holy Spirit.

Several key insights into the growth of Korean Christianity came from Dr. Won Song Ji, president of the Lutheran Church of Korea, who emphasized that statistics do not explain South Korean church growth. His first point concerned the spiritual vacuum caused by the failed efforts of the Japanese and Russians to take Korea by military force at the turn of the century. During that troubled era, the pioneering American Protestant missionaries devoted themselves immediately to health services and education, identifying themselves with Koreans in servanthood rather than top-down attitudes and strategies that mirrored those of the hated invaders. When the South was flooded with refugees from north of the 38th parallel — five million between 1945 and 1950, a high percentage of whom were Christians — they were met by Christians in the South as the main arteries of government aid in meeting survival needs. Most important, people were given hope, which, when matched with the indomitable can-do Korean spirit, bore fruit in ministries unmatched in zeal anywhere in the world. The Christian community in Korea is in a springtime of feverish planting, as well as a harvest of earlier missionary labors. As the external growth continues, Korean Christians are the first to acknowledge their need to send down deeper, more lasting roots of faith in this beleaguered peninsula off the northeast Asian continental shelf.

Visiting Japan was a homecoming for me, yet an arrival in a land vastly different from the one where I had lived in 1951. Japan was poor and struggling then, prosperous and dominant now. The door was open to Christianity then (or was it, down deep?); now the land was awash in a flood of new religions — all promoting a so-called gospel of prosperity and self-fulfillment. A symbol for the heady sense of Japanese chutzpah in conquering anything by sheer economic force was an enormous obelisk, flanked on four sides by fierce samurai warriors defying the world with swords drawn in four directions. A Japanese friend quipped that they had been unofficially renamed Honda, Toyota, Mitsubishi, and Sony. That was in Miyazaki, Japan's southernmost city, where we renewed our friendship with Naoko Ueno, who had been part of our family during her early stay in an English-language program at Concordia.

After visits to the Japan Lutheran Seminary and Lutheran Center in Tokyo, our principal visit was to the Yokohama suburb of Ofuna and the congregation I had helped begin thirty years earlier. Many of the founding members were still active, especially the Ohta family, in whose home seminarian Yoichi Imanari and I had begun Bible classes. Now they were older, as was I. Although I had been back once in the years between, this visit seemed especially meaningful, perhaps because we could not be sure that there would be a next one. Ofuna ties with Grace had grown over the years: twice Pastor Kazuteru Matsukawa had come to Grace and been a guest in our home, as well as other Japanese parishioners here on business and tourist visits. Our members had also visited there. I preached the John 3:16 text at Ofuna Lutheran Church to a congregation of about 80 on Sunday morning, far different in quantity from the Korean churches I had seen but no different in the quality of our common life in Christ.

On my visit to the seminary I renewed my friendship with Chizuo Shibata, who was now putting his early gifts of a keen mind for theology to use as a professor of theology there. He spoke with much concern about a new problem facing Japanese families: children dropping out of school, a truly baffling assault on the traditional Japanese veneration for education. The pressure to get the right education in the right school for the right job began already in kindergarten, and Shibata cited the suicide rate among youth as an alarming sign that kids were simply opting out of life in a lockstep system. Affluence was another cause of this worry: a youth with a late-model Honda bike, a Sony television, a Yamaha guitar, designer jeans, and Nike shoes did not always see discipline in school studies as worth it. I could only swap stories with him about parallels in North America.

A final visit to the Ofuna congregation before departing for home gave me a moment that was a parable of hope for the church in Japan. They gave me a Watanabe print of the *Flight to Egypt of the Holy Family*, symbolizing a tiny minority journeying through a bleak landscape. This celebrated Japanese artist painted the figures of Jesus, Mary, and Joseph in bold colors that call our attention to them rather than to the desert around them. The faces of the faithful in Ofuna stay with me to this day: a handful of worshipers who are spiritual heirs of that Holy Family, beautiful in the bright colors of faith, hope, and love. I could not have ended my sabbatical among people more dear to me.

Returning home for the Thanksgiving Day service was a joyful celebration of gratitude to God for his gracious providence throughout the sabbatical, and for the congregation, the staff, and the Feicht Fund — all of whom combined to make it possible. The congregation shared in the benefits of my sabbatical through the visits to Grace Church by twelve people I had met along the way. And the traffic was two-way: since my return, twelve Grace members have visited people and congregations who hosted me along the way. Grace has established direct mission partnerships through Andrew Miller in Kenya, Richard Matern in Nepal, and Maynard Dorow in South Korea, all of them still ongoing. The sabbatical experience has permanently deepened and broadened my vision for God's mission in his world and permeated virtually every aspect of my ministry in ways that are, indeed, more than I could ask or desire.

CHAPTER 8

Ministry Coming of Age

Maturing in ministry means an ever-deepening spiritual formation involving the whole person — body, mind, and spirit.

HENRI NOUWEN

My return from sabbatical late in 1983, and the settling in time that followed, marked a stage I would like to think of as ministry — mine and the congregation's — coming of age. The litigation with the Missouri Synod over our property ended in 1985. The church and school exterior had received a half-million-dollar facelift. The pipe organ had been renovated and expanded. Although we had already bid fond, reluctant farewells to two pillars of the staff, Victor Waldschmidt and Paul Bouman, school principal and minister of music respectively, we had welcomed Gerald Koenig and John Folkening as their capable successors. I was into my third decade of pastoral ministry at Grace Church and into my mid-fifties, with streaks of gray sprinkled through what hair was left on my head. If I was going to come of age in my vocation, this was the time.

One sign of this turn was the nature of my written communications to the congregation. For years I had written pastoral letters that were primarily newsletters with little in-depth comment on more selected aspects of the work. In 1985, when Jenny Hurrelbrink agreed to edit *Grace Notes* as a first-rate parish newsletter, I was able to make the pastoral let-ter more pastoral. I began that by giving increased attention to emerging issues of global scope in God's world that needed our awareness and prayers. In my September 1985 pastoral letter, I described two Christian leaders, one black and one white, who were in the thick of the *apartheid* struggle in South Africa. I had cited the prophetic ministries of Des-mond Tutu and Philip Beyers-Naudé in sermons; now I wrote in more detail of our ties with them through our common baptism and call to costly discipleship. I had met Tutu at a Chicago prayer breakfast and heard his witness to the power of intercessory prayer available to Chris-tians everywhere in uniting against the demonic system in South Africa. After describing the harsh realities of life for blacks in his homeland, he paused and broke into a broad smile as he held high a postcard from a monk in Alaska who was praying daily for the faithful in South Africa; he waved it over his head like a promissory note and fairly shouted, "They'll never win!" I used my pastoral letter to convey that powerful image, knowing that the people of Grace would not get it elsewhere. In the same pastoral letter, I asked Grace members to pay attention to the mounting AIDS crisis in the United States and called for our response to be something other than panic, wild speculation on how the disease spreads (I had been asked whether the communion cup was one means), or stepped-up revulsion against homosexuals who comprised three-quarters of those afflicted.

Behind that appeal was something I could not put into a pastoral let-ter. For the first time in my ministry, a Grace member had come into my office in order to "come out"; putting the matter squarely before me, he said, "I am a homosexual and want to know what you have to say about it as my pastor." He was a medical student, active in our choir, much inter-ested in theology, and conscientious in taking in all he could in Sunday adult education classes. He turned the conversation into a confessional outpouring of remorse over the sordid way of life he had explored in full but thoroughly despised. Now he longed for the community of the gos-pel. He sought neither normless promiscuity nor pretense among judg-mental Christians. He wanted Grace to be truly a community that our name implied, and so did I. He did not ask for a rewriting of the Christian faith or its moral discipline, and he counted on me for confidential, clear-headed guidance.

In continuing conversations later, we explored biblical passages on homosexuality, discerning between condition and behavior. These sessions made homosexuality anything but abstract and taught me the complexity of what goes into the condition of sexual desire for another of the same sex. My counsel to him centered in my belief that his sexuality was a condition of creation, albeit a fallen creation, and that he stood, as did I, under the judgment of the same Law on all sins of self-centered promiscuity — gay and straight alike — even as we were both redeemed by the cross of Christ to delight in God's will and walk in Christ's way. I wanted him to experience Grace Church as a community of forgiven sinners, belonging to each other under one Lord, one faith, one baptism, one God and Father of us all (Eph. 4:5-6). And he did for several years. After medical school, he moved to another city for his medical practice. We stayed in contact for some time. When I did not hear from him, I wondered. Later I learned that AIDS had taken him in his mid-thirties.

In pastoral letters I quoted correspondence from Andrew Miller's account of Kenya's President Daniel Moi's visit to Shikokho School and the encouragement of a monetary award for the excellence of its teaching staff — which included Carrie Fasholz of our congregation. In a letter of late August 1985, I reminded our members of meeting Margaret Chang in China two years earlier and the fruition of plans for her to come as our guest. Something of the flavor of her invincible faith came through in a letter she wrote to our members:

> Praised be God for all His lovingkindness to me, because He has done wonders for me in years past and still does! He has helped me to perform everything which concerned my procedure successfully of coming to the States. It is really a miracle, and He is using your Feicht Memorial Fund so directly in enabling me to come to be with you at Grace Church this fall. His presence is with me wherever I go. I went to Shanghai on July 9th, especially for my passport extension. The consular officer gave me the per-

mission and I returned to Soochow the next day. In spite of very hot weather my Lord increased my strength on the way. How grateful I am to Him!

As it turned out, that pastoral letter was the only way Grace members could meet Margaret: she died suddenly only a few days before her scheduled departure. If she could have come, she would have told the fascinating story of her seventy years in China to every group at Grace, including Genesis, a recently formed fellowship of members whose birthdays preceded the 1929 date on the cornerstone of Grace Church. Among those who would have delighted in listening to Margaret was a member who was just beginning to find her way into her new world as a widow. Myrtle Staver was initially hesitant about attending a Genesis meeting, but she worked up the courage to come anyway. Her letter to me was one I wanted all our members to read, and with her permission I excerpted this sentence as a sign of what a congregation can be: "I was by myself, but at a table where two others came I had not met before. I want you to know that meant so much to me and I look forward to the next time."

In previous pastoral letters I had simply announced the dates and times of a new adult instruction classes without giving reasons for Grace members to recognize the critical importance of their personal outreach to others. Several weeks before the fall series of instruction classes in 1986, I took several paragraphs of the pastoral letter to tell the story of Neil, whose funeral I had conducted a short time before — with three people attending. He died of heroin addiction, a young man of 31, born, raised, and schooled in River Forest. He was the boy next door who once rode his bike on our streets and hung out with kids at the mall. But who, I asked, ever asked what his home life was like or ever reached out to him and his family with an invitation to church? No parent or family member was at his funeral, signifying the sheer bleakness of a life that ended so soon, without ever being reached or being cared about enough to come into the welcoming arms of Christ through a welcome from his people. I did not tell the Neil story, however, as a sentimental tug on the heartstrings; it was an admonition to the people of Grace to recognize the mission around the corner as well as around the world.

Pastoral letters were also an occasion to encourage members to faithfully use their gifts, in some cases the gift of writing. In my January 1986 pastoral letter, I saluted Melvin Holli and briefly described the contents of two books he had coming out that year on the ethnic and political history of Chicago. Few of us knew that one of our Grace School mothers, Ruth El Saffar, was an author and scholar of international acclaim on the seventeenth-century writer Cervantes. I told of her five books, the most recent of which was *Beyond Fiction,* her plea to lift up the beauty and power of literature without floundering in the morass of literary theory. Stephen Schmidt wrote an *apologia* for Lutheran teachers. Don Heimburger's book told the story of Midwestern railroads. Jill Baumgaertner was a published poet and recognized authority on Flannery O'Connor; in addition, her textbook on literature was used widely on college campuses. I was proud of these people and described their work as a response to St. Paul's praise of "whatever is honorable, whatever is just, whatever is pure, whatever is excellent and gracious . . ." (Phil. 4:8). I should have included two of my own books that were published during the mid-1980s, one on the art of preaching and the other a book of sermons, if for no other reason than to indicate that I was practicing what I preached.

I grew to genuinely enjoy writing pastoral letters as an integral part of my ministry's coming of age, and I valued the privilege of entering 850 homes via the printed word at least once, often twice a month. I knew that they were read because the feedback was sometimes critical, though more often it was appreciative. It told me that a carefully written pastoral letter had the power to make our parish life *interesting* — as life together under the risen Lord surely is. I intended them to be a channel of deeper levels of relationship between pastor and people, part of my ministry coming of age. I wrote them with care because language matters. The magnificent sweep of biblical imagery from the Psalms, Job, Isaiah 40–66, Luke 1 and 2, the Sermon on the Mount, 1 Corinthians 13, and elsewhere were a motivation to work and rework pastoral letters and sermons to clear out the clutter and vitalize my prose for people who deserved the best from me. During those years I expanded my reading beyond religious journals *(The Christian Century, Theology To-*

day, The International Review of Missions, Word and World, Context) to include *Atlantic, Harper's,* and *The New Yorker,* magazines whose literary excellence matched their content. It was an era when language in American culture in general had gone into a steep coarsening, dumbing-down trend; I believed that this made our calling at Grace all the more urgent to speak in a different voice. I regret not drawing more widely on fiction to enrich what I had to say and how to say it. But much of my reading was late in the evening after a full day's work; or it may have been that my Lutheran sense of guilt about the use of time was at work.

In January 1986, I invited all members to a Parish Day to review where we had been more recently and to think together about future directions. It did not surprise me that, out of a parish of 1,766 baptized souls, only 45 showed up. And these were mostly elected officers and staff of Grace, to whom I had sent special invitations. The focus of the day was on the overall ministry of the congregation and school and the matter of adequate staffing to support our work. Despite the relatively low turnout, that Saturday brought important insights and suggestions. The elders and I reviewed the feedback of the day carefully, looking in particular for trends discerned over the thirty years since 1955. There was modest but steady growth to report — an 8 percent increase in baptized membership. Attendance at Holy Communion had increased since the Eucharist was offered more frequently. Sunday morning attendance had decreased, however, a sign of the increase of competing activities. Those distractions were particularly felt in the drop in Sunday school attendance from 456 children enrolled in 1955 to 140 in 1986. The Men's Club had disappeared altogether, and the Women's Society had decreased in size, reflecting the sharp increase in women working outside the home and men wanting more evenings at home.

Laypeople were much more visible as participants in Sunday worship as lectors and assistants in communion distribution, and more women were active as members of the church council and voters' assemblies each month. Youth ministry was lagging behind the mid-1950s level of high-school youth participation. Fewer members were being received by transfer, but a greater percentage were joining Grace via adult

instruction. The congregation was more homogeneous racially and eth-
nically in 1955; now, in 1986, the greater diversity was both a blessing
and a challenge. Children were less likely to follow the spiritual path of
their parents; young adults new to the community tended to come to
Grace not because we or they were Lutheran but because they were in
search of spiritual roots and friendship to fill the gaps of urban loneli-
ness. Expectations of pastoral ministry were more exacting, particularly
in pastoral counseling. In 1955 our offerings totaled $148,700; in 1985,
they had grown to $809,600, an increase of 540 percent. Inflation not-
withstanding, those statistics showed an incremental growth in stewardship.

Reflection on these trends moved us toward staffing in several new
areas. The financial/business side of the congregation had outgrown the
willing volunteer work of church treasurers and elected financial officers. We had recently received a taste of the quality of upgraded service
in this area from Al Guemmer, a retired executive from the Wrigley Cor-
poration who volunteered several days a week. In short order he provided
needed improvement to our finance and business-management systems.
We would gladly have kept Al longer, but his family move to Florida
meant we had to look beyond volunteers. The parish decided to establish
the position of business manager and chose Beth McClory on a twenty-
hour-per-week employment basis, the first of a series of business managers. She walked into a welter of tasks that awaited her arrival: office space
renovation, new boilers, heat conservation, asbestos removal, and the
changeover to computers. Putting her business experience to work, Beth
waded in fearlessly. A former teacher on our staff, Wendy Will, was chosen to work as ministry coordinator, a new and untried but needed position to enable members to find their niche in belonging and serving in a
rapidly changing congregation. Wendy brought energy and high commitment to her tasks as a "people-person"; plus, she had the advantage of
being well known by many school families as a teacher of their children.

I took a personal hand in these staff developments and supported
each one of them wholeheartedly. But I assumed too much. The simple
act of adding positions needed a greater perception on my part of the
changing culture of the staff and the congregation. No longer were the

staple figures of Vic Waldschmidt and Paul Bouman on hand to carry out their responsibilities of school and music — with little attention from my side. The key to pastoral administration was not assuming things would run smoothly as before, but in discerning how effectively each colleague applied the gifts he or she had for the overall good, so that the gospel could come through clearly in our ministry to the congregation. To that end, we met as a staff every Monday morning, began Wednesdays with worship together, and held a staff retreat late in August every year. Yet it was a challenge, and it dawned on me during those years that my ministry's coming of age had new dimensions of applying both Law and Gospel, admonition and support, critique and commendation in ways that I had not known before.

Earlier in the 1980s, initiatives by our assistant pastor, James Wind, had brought together many of the medical professionals at Grace to explore the spiritual core of their work as doctors and nurses. The first problem was to find a time when these busy people could meet. Saturday afternoons from 3:00 to 5:00 worked best. Jim and I, together with neurosurgeon Douglas Anderson and nurse educator Linda Bernard, worked up guideline materials that framed the early discussions from Scripture and medical sources for the deeper meaning of healing and wellness. We sought insight into the distinctions between curing and healing: the former refers to bodily restoration to health, the latter to the broader wholeness of body, soul, and mind. Several dozen joined these late Saturday afternoon sessions. One surprise to me was how quickly the agenda moved from abstract discussion to concrete experiences. Doctors and nurses opened up about their dilemma of having nowhere to go in the clinical setting with accidental mistakes that could cost their patients added pain, expense, and sometimes their lives. To talk of such things openly in the professional setting was taboo, ruled out by the litigious climate that could end medical careers with insurmountable legal costs. One nurse spoke of carrying a burden of guilt for twenty years because the attending physician had ordered her to administer a lethal dosage of medicine to a terminal patient — and then left her alone with her dilemma. All of them spoke of the pressure from families of patients, whose expectations of doctors and nurses reached god-like proportions.

Conflict between medical professionals was another problem our members spoke of — the petty jealousies, jockeying for status, and communication breakdowns that made sin all too apparent in their daily vocations. Wind and I were discovering that these caregivers needed healing no less than their patients did. Those Saturday afternoons became a safe place for people in medicine to find a new awareness of the healing offered Sunday after Sunday, the confession and absolution that began every Communion liturgy. As trust deepened, the men and women of this support group gave each other the mutual ministry of what the Lutheran Confessions call "the mutual conversation and consolation of believers." Honesty about professional dilemmas could be aired without threat or judgment. Ministry was coming of age through a congregation becoming more of a place of healing for the healers.

This took place about the same time that Lutheran General Hospital in Park Ridge began an exploratory venture of bringing clergy, medical professionals, and ethicists together from around the country and abroad — known as Project Ten. I was glad for the invitation to join others from Grace to contribute what we were learning on Saturday afternoons. George Caldwell, chief administrator at Lutheran General, had the vision, skill, and financial clout to annually convene this group of several dozen gifted people, and I suspect that the Marcos Island, Florida, venue helped attendance. It gave me an opportunity to meet people in medicine and ethics who became friends as well as contributors to my expanding vision of the congregation as a place of healing. The Park Ridge Center in Chicago, a research institute on the intersection of faith, medicine, and ethics, grew out of Project Ten, and my pastoral ties to its program continued throughout the remaining years of my ministry at Grace. I was glad for the participation of Grace members David Stein and Marion Miller on the staff, and for Martin Marty's visionary gifts in founding this center and advancing its purposes.

Those Saturday afternoon sessions had another important outcome. The experience with doctors and nurses encouraged us to turn the focus toward people in and beyond the congregation with chronic illness. Stephen Schmidt stepped forward as the ideal leader: he had battled and was still battling Crohn's Disease, and he had the leadership skills as a teacher and theologian to bring together people who needed what the group offered, the mutual ministry of faith, prayer, shared experience, and the strength that comes from telling each other the truth. Thus the Chronic Illness Group came into being in the mid-1980s. Sophie Wright was one of the pillars of the group from early on. She had come to the United States from Poland as a teenager and World War II refugee, studied nursing, joined Grace, and then qualified for the Chronic Illness Group as a cancer battler. She provided a barley-bread kind of earthy inspiration, admonition, humor, compassion, and faith in the monthly gatherings that drew Grace members and others of all ages and ailments. Another strong witness in the group was Steve Koos, who joined Grace in 1981 with his wife and two sons, and not long afterward came down with Gardner's Syndrome, a rare chronic disease that he fought for four years. Throughout this time, he gave and received remarkable spiritual and moral support. I asked him to tell his story of living with dying to a large gathering of people from a number of parishes on the Friday after Easter 1988, and no one missed a word of his quiet, humor-tinged, unshakable witness. Just a few weeks before his death the following September, he and his wife, Sharon, had the grace to help a new refugee family with an appliance they could spare from their home. At his funeral, the church was filled with people he had blessed, including a full contingent of the Chronic Illness Group. I can think of no group in the parish for which the classic Lutheran term "the priesthood of all believers" was a better fit. Stephen Schmidt has continued to provide guidance, but the group leads itself as participants share experience, prayer, struggle, victories, doubts, recoveries, relapses, life, and death. Schmidt based his book *The Congregation as a Place of Healing* on the journey shared by that group. There, indeed, ministry was coming of age among people who saw the miracle, not of disease cured, but of healing that comes from the strength of Christ's love to bear, believe, hope, and endure all things.

Our experience with medical people and the chronically ill cultivated a readiness during those middle years of the 1980s to take the promise of God's varied ways of healing to the whole congregation. Beginning on St. Luke's Day, October 18, 1985, we introduced a Service of the Word for Healing and continued it on evenings spaced at quarterly intervals throughout the year. The reason we did not offer it on Sunday mornings was our timidity about the whole idea of healing, plus our lack of maturity in recognizing its central place in the ministry of Jesus. Our reluctance stemmed from a culture of privatizing illllness, bearing it stoically as a stigma, and suspecting faith healers were fakes. But we learned from fellow members who were in the Chronic Illness Group; for a decade they had shaken off these traditional blinders. After I had prepared the parish in pastoral letters that focused on the forgiveness of sins as the heart of healing and explained the voluntary act of coming forward for anointing as part of Holy Communion, we introduced it on a Sunday morning. Nearly the entire congregation participated, and once again I learned not to underestimate the readiness of Christians to take a new step of faith when well prepared. The Service of the Word for Healing continues at Grace Church at stated intervals throughout the year.

Why this move toward corporate participation in the Lord's grace of healing should have come so slowly and only gradually over those years puzzled me. In hospital calls and home visits to the sick, I cannot count the times I had turned to Matthew 9:1-8 for the truth about healing as one inclusive work of Christ for body and soul. As Grace Church had learned the hard way during the 1970s, congregations as well as whole denominations get sick and become places that wound rather than heal. Pastoral ministry can be a part of the ailment or an instrument of healing. Our experience enduring the blight of denominational sickness in the 1970s, followed by the boon of the congregation as a place of healing in the '80s, were back-to-back contrasts that came home forcefully to me, making me regret the former and appreciate the latter.

Throughout this decade opportunities came to widen my pastoral ministry through writing. I inherited from my predecessor, Otto Geiseman, the practice of sending my sermons to those who wished to receive them as home-bound members, students away at school, or members in military service, as well as former members who simply wanted a connection to the Grace pulpit. I developed an odd habit in this connection: every Monday morning, my first activity was to rewrite the sermon I had preached the day before. Though odd, it was a good discipline, and not a few times did I finish the manuscript with a sigh that I'd finally gotten it right. The custom of writing and rewriting sermons made for an easy transition to publishing them as *In Season,* for pastoral subscribers throughout the nation, many of whom are in places where collegial opportunities for preparing sermons are lacking. The risk in publishing sermons, of course, is that they are misused: instead of using them to prime the pump, the preacher uses them as a substitute for his or her own work. Only once have I been a guest in a congregation where that happened. I was worshiping in Palm Desert, California, and I recognized my sermon from the first sentence. At the end of the service I shook the pastor's hand without mentioning my name. I'm sure the brother had a week of overload with crises of every sort.

In 1981, I began a four-year term of service as the pastoral member of the board of the Association of Theological Schools, the accrediting organization for the Protestant and Catholic seminaries in the United States. That meant two-day trips twice a year to Dayton, Ohio, where Jesse Ziegler and later Leon Pacala served as the executive director, with Marvin Taylor and David Schuller as key associates. These were people who had their fingers on the pulse of American seminary education as no others did, and being with them and the seminary educators on the board gave me a window of greater understanding of theological education among the 50,000 or more seminarians in the land, among whom nearly one-half were women. I could serve on this board because as the one parish pastor member I was not required to make extended visits to seminary campuses, something I had neither the qualifications nor the time for. Hearing the reports and entering the discussions also made me appreciate the quality of my own seminary education at Concordia in St. Louis. As was true of my membership on other boards, what I had to contribute to the Association of Theological Schools came directly from my home base at Grace Church.

Another opportunity that broadened my pastoral work was the invitation to teach twice a year at Maxwell Air Force Base School for Chaplains near Birmingham, Alabama. It was an altogether new setting for me, since I had never served in the armed forces myself, but it was beneficial in the contacts I made with chaplains serving American service personnel all over the world. My subjects were preaching and pastoral care, both of which provided crosswalks between civilian and military congregations in ways that made sense for me to be there. On occasion I was given a closer look at the F-16 fighter planes lined up on the tarmac, as well as the bombers that looked as lethal as the load they delivered. I did not know enough about these aircraft to ask intelligent questions, and the answers probably would have been vague anyway, since classified data was not available to civilians. But I could not help thinking that for the cost of every fighter plane, a dozen Grace Churches could be built, and for the bombers triple that number. In addition to the ATS and Maxwell AFB trips twice a year, I continued to serve on the board of the Academy of Parish Clergy and enjoyed the annual convocations with friends and colleagues in ministry whom I had known since its founding in 1968. All these contacts expanded my horizons. What made the privilege of participating extra good was the support of the congregation and its understanding that these times away from Grace brought me back home better for my calling.

In the early 1980s I received a letter from a local clinical psychologist, inviting clergy to join him for a lunch and conversation exploring whether there were enough common ties between us to warrant meeting together with some regularity. Richard Matteson made a positive impression on me immediately. He was an ordained Methodist minister, with parish experience, who had moved over to a vocation of psychological counseling after finishing the doctoral work that qualified him for it. It was good to continue conversations with him, and I wondered why so few other clergy in town recognized the potential of the partnership. We soon began monthly lunch hours together for the purpose of exchanging insights into the problems of people we were both counseling — always with the permission of the person involved. It was a boon for me to know Matteson as one to whom I could refer people with emotional-mental problems beyond my scope (panic attacks would be a common example). He in turn referred to me people with no spiritual bearings in order for them to receive God's ways of healing the soul, so inextricably intertwined with the mind and body. Dozens of our members benefited from this combined approach, and to my knowledge no single person felt exploited by the fact that we helped each other help them. In the winter of 1986, I invited Matteson to lead ten Thursday evening sessions on the "Family in Christian Perspective," sponsored by the Feicht Fund. It was the first of many adult education offerings he led at Grace in the following years. His partnership contributed much to my counseling ministry, which increased significantly during the decade of the 1980s; and often enough during our regular lunch hours, we were a source of counsel and consolation to each other.

Other events of note in my 1980s ministry at Grace included sponsoring more refugee families, this time working with couples and families from Bulgaria and Romania who were among the rising tide of people crossing into western Europe at the risk of their lives. A support group for single mothers began in 1987, and Beverly and I were glad to have eight of them with their children for a long camping weekend on Detroit Island. Hymn festivals became an annual event in the latter half of the decade, often combined with an ice cream social on the church lawn on the hottest evening of the summer. Evelyn and Alvin Haase celebrated their fiftieth wedding anniversary with a generous endowment of a fund for the enrichment of the ministry of music at Grace Church. Appeals for drought relief in East Africa received generous response during that crisis in the spring and summer of 1984.

Guenther Gutgesell announced his decision to retire at the end of 1988, after having been the head janitor at Grace for almost thirty years and something of a legend on our staff. He was born in Germany and was for a time a prisoner of war before World War II ended. In 1956 he arrived with Rosemarie, joining his Uncle Felix to take care of our building as if it were his own. He drove our Grace School bus for many years without an accident; no child would dare challenge his German-style, no-nonsense rules when riding to and from school. Guenther was loved by the kids, by parishioners and staff, and not the least by me. As his farewell gift to the congregation, he painted the entire interior of the sanctuary by himself; when it was all done, he asked me to come into the chancel to kneel for a prayer of thanksgiving. His send-off party was a gala, with no speech coming close to his own hilarious recollections of years past.

During the 1980s our giving pattern changed little year by year, with a quarter of the budget still coming in during the December push. We had our first Jazz Liturgy in 1988, written by Andy Tecson and sung by Carol Olsen and Douglas Anderson, accompanied by a first-rate jazz trio. And on a fine post-Easter Sunday in that year the congregation surprised me with a celebration of the twenty-fifth anniversary of my installation, done in the best of taste and with a warmth of spirit that filled my heart to overflowing.

Earlier that spring we held a leadership retreat for the purpose of giving our parish constitution a major overhaul. Assistant Pastor Peter Marty was the point man in seeing the committee through the many meetings needed to come up with a framework that fit our mission and ministry as we looked toward the last decade of the twentieth century and into the next millennium. I was grateful for Peter's talent and forbearance in staying with a task that did not stir my soul but was of primary importance nonetheless. Two major changes resulted: the first was the removal of any barrier that prevented women from serving in any office of the congregation, including that of elder; the second was the tripling (from 30 to 90) of the number of elective offices for lay leadership. The increased lay participation on key boards reflected the fact that Grace Church was extraordinarily blessed with people gifted for many forms of service, and it was time to open the way for much wider use of those gifts. The new charter also changed a seventy-year-old custom of electing a chairman at each congregational meeting; now a president would be elected to serve a three-year term in that role. I remember Ron Kindelsperger's inspired speech of gratitude at a Sunday morning post-worship message to the congregation as he took office. He recalled entering Grace as a kindergarten child, never thinking that the day would come when he would occupy the position to which he was now elected. Another sign of the recognition of lay leadership was that the pastor no longer chaired the meetings of the church council; that now fell under the duties of the president. After sitting in that chair for twenty-five years, I had no problem at all turning those responsibilities over to people gifted for it. In my theology, that was also a sign of equipping God's people for service, and thus of my ministry's coming of age.

We had one more major step to take in 1988. The assistant pastor program, which had been in place since 1948 and had blessed the sixteen of us who had participated in it, was to end in two years. In 1990, the congregation would call an associate pastor, with no term of service stipulated in the call. I had advocated all these steps and had said so publicly. It had become increasingly difficult to bring graduates from Seminex for ordination and two years of service. And the widened scope of pastoral ministry at Grace called for more sustained pastoral help for me. I had been the beneficiary — immensely so — of the assistant pastors from 1963 onward, and knew I would miss the stimulation of their partnership in ministry, brief though it was. It also made me regret that they would no longer take the leaven of their Grace years to new places of their calling. But it was time to make the change.

The list of previous assistant pastors now serving elsewhere was impressive. Richard Gotsch was in parish ministry in Northbrook to the north of us; Paul Firnhaber was in California; Stanley Bahn was in Appleton, Wisconsin; Philip Bruening was in Richmond, Virginia; Ronald Rentner, all seven feet of him, was in urban ministry in the San Francisco Bay area; Frank Janzow was in suburban Milwaukee; Aaron Sorrels was in Michigan; James Wind had joined the staff of the Park Ridge Center, later the Lilly Foundation staff, and after that became president of the Alban Institute, the premier research center on congregations in America; David Schreiber was in Indianapolis; Arthur Going was in a suburb of Atlanta; Peter Marty was in Kansas City, and later would move to a key congregation in Davenport, Iowa. Soon Arndt Braaten would join us as the twelfth assistant to be my partner at Grace.

Dietrich Bonhoeffer once coined the phrase "the world come of age," meaning the secular realm claiming an autonomy of its own, independent of God. For me, the coming of age of my ministry meant the opposite. This was a time of a seasoning of my life ever more formed in Jesus Christ, a maturing of the ministry given me by the Holy Spirit, and a deepening of love for the people who gave me reason to thank God daily for the privilege of serving them at Grace Lutheran Church.

CHAPTER 9

Continuities, Endings, Beginnings

And the end of all our exploring
Will be to arrive where we started
And know the place for the first time.

T. S. ELIOT

As the 1990s arrived, the thought of retirement occasionally crossed my mind, but it did as a distant cloud on the far horizon rather than anything suggesting an immediate winding down of my ministry. If anything, I was more given to cranking up for the new decade that was beginning, in the manner of the advice a high-school track coach once gave me for running the 220-yard dash: "Go as fast as you can for the first hundred and gradually increase your speed." Leon Rosenthal had accepted the call as associate pastor at Grace and was installed in late September of 1990. He came to us well experienced in pastoral ministry and with a doctorate from the University of Chicago. We worked together in serving a Grace Church that was alive and well in new directions of ministry. While it was not easy for me to divide the preaching half and half, it was important to do so as part of the plan to free me for more time in counseling and administering the expanding work at Grace.

Twelve new parish programs were underway. Helpmates brought

single and divorced people together on Monday nights. People to People was started as a cadre of some forty members on call for emergency help to people with varying needs. Tapestry was an imaginative program that brought parishioners together monthly around common interests, hobbies, and travel experiences. Grace Members at Work began during this time as a support group for those who had recently lost their jobs and soon broadened its vision to wider issues of ethics in the workplace, with links to the Center for Ethics and Corporate Policy in Chicago. This group also took on the sponsorship of taping Sunday services and delivering the videos to homebound members; they also took the videos to local cable stations for broadcast to audiences throughout the Chicago area. Children who had lost parents through death or divorce were welcomed for friendship, fun, and counsel after school by well-qualified members in our version of Rainbows for All God's Children, a national program begun by Catholics. Grace members also volunteered as literacy teachers of inmates at the Cook County Jail. Tentmakers was a new venture in high-school youth leadership that trained post-college Lutheran adults to serve youth part-time while holding other jobs. The Prayer Chain coordinated members who covenanted for intercessory prayer for all who asked for it. Center Aisle was the name chosen for the latest form of fellowship and service among young single adults, so named because the center aisle at Grace was often the gathering place for those who welcomed the company of others for post-service brunch instead of the rest of Sunday alone. These burgeoning activities, often initiated by laity who had the heart for them and felt the need for them, were gathered together under the umbrella of the Board of Fellowship and Service, which worked as a switchboard coordinating services and scheduling building space. The squeeze on meeting space for these and other functions at Grace was a good sign of the vitality of the Spirit at work among us. It was also one of the reasons I had so few evenings at home.

In the autumn of 1991, I made a lunch date with Ken Hartmann, a Grace member and attorney who had been invaluable during our litigation years and with whom I had often enjoyed lunch conversations on a wide range of subjects. In the course of that conversation he happened to mention a tent sale staged annually in the Catholic parish his wife attended, a huge event that brought people and cash together in impressive numbers. It struck me that the time might be right for something similar at Grace, and a month later I called together four couples of the parish for dessert and coffee at the parsonage. The Beckers, Claussens, Schupkegels, Zyers, and later the Krouts, were the thirties-something kind of people who needed to know that their time had come to be part of a new generation of leaders. None of them were longtime Grace members; all of them brought unique stories of spiritual journeys that led them to Grace Church and School.

David and Connie Zyer were good examples. She had lost both her parents earlier in her life, but had carried on with a strong faith. In meeting and marrying David, she showed patience in putting no pressure on her husband while he took two years of careful reflecting on the basics of the Lutheran tradition before he joined the congregation. I had come to know and admire them while preparing them for their wedding at Grace Church not too many years before. To my knowledge, the couples I chose did not know each other well, but they symbolized a generation of high promise that had not yet recognized their potential for keeping the congregation from growing old before its time. And I was sure they were savvy enough to figure out that my invitation to the parsonage was for more than dessert. I asked them to hear me out on the idea of a Grace Church Tent Sale; and after they all spoke of being too busy, I made my case that their youth, energy, imagination, and readiness for challenge were why I asked them to consider it. They went home, put it in their thoughts and prayers, and came back with the good news that they were game to try.

What came about seven months later was a tent sale that exceeded anything we imagined. Five hundred parishioners became involved in preparing and staging the two-day event late in May 1992, which put twenty sale booths under brightly colored tents on the Concordia grounds west of the church. On the morning of the first day of the sale, I photographed the gates opening and hundreds of people racing for booths of their choice, something like a latter-day mini-version of the Oklahoma land rush. Another sight that stayed with me was that of a trial attorney who had never taken hold of Grace membership in any meaningful way patiently helping a person paw through a rack of used men's suits to find the right color and fit, and striking up a conversation about the unusual circumstances that brought them together as members of the same congregation. The leadership talent that surfaced in those months was symbolized by the thick notebook of lists, assignments, reports, charts, permits, and logistics of all kinds that the leadership team had put together. The prime value of the half-year experience of working together was reflected in a celebration picnic after the tent sale that featured one testimony after another by those who had discovered through working together the grace of new friendships, increased ownership in the congregation, the use of talents previously unknown, and the genuine fun of it all. From the beginning we had decided that the profits would go beyond our own general fund. The recipients of checks for $20,000 each were the Circle Ministry in Chicago's Austin area, Walther Lutheran High School, and Grace School. Later versions of the Grace Tent Sale followed, leaving a trail of goodwill, good support, and Grace Tent Sale T-shirts in their wake.

As 1992 approached, the congregation approved the adoption of the Stephen Ministry program to provide more training for members who wanted more depth as lay participants in what Lutherans sometimes called *seelsorge,* the care of souls. The term had traditionally referred to pastoral care, but a Missouri Synod pastor, Stephen Haugk, had pioneered a new direction of training lay helpers to extend the care of Jesus to those burdened with woes of every sort. Wendy Will accepted the challenge of training Grace participants in the required fifty hours of instruction, as well as the challenge of training the congregation to understand the program and calling on Stephen Ministers as needs arose. Within two years, fourteen were quietly at work in the parish; six years later the number of those trained and serving had reached thirty-five.

A phone call in the autumn of 1991 from a woman representing a suburban group that was seeking churches as homeless shelters seemed innocent enough, but it began a venture that had far more explosive consequences than I realized at the time. I was aware of the plight of suburban homeless people from thirty-five years of hearing their stories and attempting to muster some form of help. But I underestimated how adamantly fearful and resolutely opposed some neighbors, including some Grace parishioners, were to cooperating with other congregations in establishing overnight shelters. I met with people from Tri-Village PADS (Public Action to Deliver Shelter) and invited Dan Lehmann, our congregation president, to join in the meeting. Would we consider being a one-night-per-week shelter for homeless men, women, and children? Biblical passages such as Isaiah 58:6 ("share your bread with the hungry and bring the homeless poor into your house") told us that we'd better be open to the idea rather than too conveniently busy with other things. We took the appeal to our Social Ministry Committee, which recommended positively to the church council, where similar approval was given after we provided more education about the shelter program and the needs it met. Finally, after a year of open meetings, heated pro-and-con debate, opinions from the River Forest town board that zoning ordinances forbade shelters, and increasing press coverage of our parish struggle, we staggered through to a Yes decision by a strong majority.

On the Sunday morning after that decision, worshipers coming to Grace for the 8:30 service were greeted by something never seen before in our parish history: picketers were on the church steps distributing leaflets, fear-mongering misinformation printed on glo-orange paper. I was upset but not surprised to see one of our members among them, and I asked them to stop. This got nowhere. Then I sent senior elder Carol Domrose out to talk to the picketers. She was a Christian of unimpeachable integrity, firmness, and clear-headed commitment — or as the children who were her River Forest elementary school pupils would put it, "Don't mess with this lady." She got the job done. I preached the Isaiah 58 text appointed for the day with no reference to the picketers, whose tactics did not need my censure from the pulpit. The Fellowship Hall was packed for the special meeting of the congregation that followed that 11 a.m. service, much the same in mood and number as fifteen years earlier during the heat of the LCMS struggle. The council's recommendation to approve Grace as a shelter site was passed resoundingly in a meeting that was much shorter than many had anticipated. Chicago television reporters, who were waiting outside the building, interviewed Grace parishioners as they filed out. The best one-line summary on the evening news came from Adrian Rott: "Today love and fear collided, and love won." The congregation's decision to participate in the PADS program meant half the battle was won.

The other half was with the River Forest Village Board. In open hearings that filled the meeting room with neighbors, most of them vehemently against any homeless shelter in River Forest, Grace members George and Betty Moore were among the faithful advocates and Richard Martens brought important support as an attorney. I hated those meetings, and as they dragged on for months, I realized that I had erred in not motivating more Grace parishioners to educate their neighbors that sheltering two dozen people in our Fellowship Hall, mothers and children among them, was no dire threat at all. But when real estate values are placed above human values, the reaction can be uglier than I was prepared for, and those meetings became a lesson in the sins of suburbia. Seen in that light, I reluctantly accepted the public hearings as opportunities for public ministry and bore witness to our sheltering homeless people as an extension of our obedience as a congregation to the Word of God. Accordingly, the civil government could not forbid an intrinsically religious action according to the First Amendment, with its free exercise of religion clause. The River Forest town board could and did pass ordinances that required us to meet what we regarded as excessive standards to provide supper, a mattress, and breakfast the next morning for people who were regularly referred to as "the element from Chicago and Maywood" — code language for poor blacks and poor whites alike.

It was our location in an upper-class suburb with a platinum reputation that drew the media coverage for months. During that time, however, my public ministry through testimony and articles in the press gave me a channel of witness to a River Forest not known by the stereotypes about it. I received letters and occasional calls from River Forest residents who were people of civic righteousness and moral courage, and their support greatly encouraged me. Another boon was forging a much deeper friendship with Rabbi Victor Mirelman of the nearby Har Zion Synagogue. We met together often, commiserated, strategized, and grew to be partners in carrying out the message of the biblical prophets in a setting more volatile than our respective sanctuaries provided.

We took our turn at Grace Church as the Saturday night shelter from the autumn of 1991 through the spring of 1992. Then, in a decision that troubled me because it was too quick in moving to provisional housing for homeless people, we discontinued our place in the rotation of overnight shelters in churches. The troubling thing was that provisional housing was being provided only by the Family Service social agency in Oak Park, and while it was excellent as far as it went, it could not go far enough in serving vast numbers of suburban homeless. I had become well acquainted with the Family Service and Mental Health Agency of Oak Park and River Forest through joining its board of directors during this time. It opened my eyes to the mental health needs in both communities that I had never known before, and it introduced me to people who gave generously of their time and talents as board members in monthly meetings, which were over by 9 a.m., thus allowing me to fit board membership into my work schedule at Grace. What I had not counted on, however, was the serious disarray of finances and the agency administration problems in this agency that was nearly a century old. David Strom and Patrick Staunton were of particular help during my two-year term as board president, when it became necessary to dismiss the senior agency staff and find replacements. The lessons I had learned about leadership through church and community conflicts were useful as the board worked hard to secure the needed financial and moral support of the community to keep the agency alive. We not only survived, but we came through stronger in appreciation of how a community, board, and staff can rally to turn a crisis into an improved institution of service. My tenure on the Family Service board was not time off from my Grace Church calling; it was part of my larger service to God, whose providence was at work in the community through this agency that served people with broken minds and hearts.

As the ups and downs of congregation and public ministry went on through the first half of the 1990s, the routines of my daily work at Grace had moments that taught me not to take everydayness for granted. In a pastoral letter I related an experience, one of the God-given surprises that come along when least expected and most needed. A young mother came knocking at my study door, tired and rumpled from nights spent with her husband and two children sleeping in their car. I had heard hundreds of hard-luck stories over the years, but somehow the weariness in her face and the presence of her two children told me that she was new at begging and embarrassed to ask for the $40 to cover the cost of brake parts that her husband was out trying to buy for the car. I explained that normally the church gave food or clothing, but not money because of the frequency of its misuse for drugs or alcohol. She listened, nodded silently in assent, and was about to turn away when I asked her where they were headed. She reached into her purse for an identification tag with a Wisconsin home and phone number, and she asked me to call and verify it if I would. The children were tugging at her arm for something to eat while this conversation took place, and I thought of the church refrigerator that contained leftovers from a supper the night before. I took them to the kitchen for food, and while they were eating, I returned to my study to figure out what to do next. The mail had just arrived, and in it was a letter from a parishioner who wanted to show gratitude to God for mercies received; two twenty-dollar bills were enclosed with the letter, and the request that we use the money as we saw fit. My pastoral letter described what happened when the mother and her children returned from their meal:

> I told the mother that I had just received a letter from a grateful person with an enclosure of forty dollars — the amount needed to fix the car — that even I couldn't miss as a sign of the Lord's timing and generosity. A new look of hope came into those tired eyes, even as her two children's faces were brightened by the food they had just enjoyed. Off they went. Was I taken in by a smooth con artist working the church beat? Did the money go for brake parts? I don't know. I do know that two hungry kids and a weary mom were fed. I do know that the Wisconsin phone number she gave me checked out. I do know that Christ was served, named, and honored. I left it all in his hands, from whence come our daily

blessings even without our prayers. Here in our small corner of the vineyard where we live, you and I meet the Christ who calls us to care for so many more like this family in and beyond our land.

Experiences like this, plus the provisional nature of emergency shelter for homeless people, made me realize the need for our congregation to engage in more than stopgap measures. To be sure, every time the Word was proclaimed, the sacraments received, the prayers and doxologies of worship offered up, we were about the Father's business with more than stopgap measures. And the presence of every baptized person in the daily life of home, work, and community meant that the leaven of Christ's presence was there, recognized or not. Nevertheless, we needed to be more intentional in finding ways to do our part in preventing as well as curing the besetting ailments in life all around us.

In January 1990, Grace Church formed the Social Concerns Ministry. Its mandate was to provide information, to educate, and to enable involvement in working toward solutions to social problems immediate to our community. Galen Gockel, a professor of urban studies and an experienced political officeholder, chaired the committee of nine members and announced the focus on housing/homelessness and hunger/nutrition as the focus of the group. The homeless shelter program at Grace was one form of response; but the committee worked to broaden ties with other church agencies and congregations that offered valuable experience from which we could learn. We established regular support for three area food pantries, and continued for years with a collection box for canned food placed prominently in our narthex.

In addition to our decade of ties with the Chicago Uptown Ministry, we began another ministry program — this time with Holy Family Lutheran congregation and school in Chicago's Cabrini Green. Pastor Charles Infeldt was a friend and pastoral colleague with whom I often met; he was somehow always upbeat about the miracle of Holy Family in the midst of one of the nation's toughest public housing areas. He and his Swedish-born wife were the most improbable couple one could imagine in that neighborhood, but they simply never gave up on the reality of a

Lutheran school in a part of the city long vacated by Lutheran congregations and schools. Early on, the Social Concerns Committee advocated Grace Church support for Holy Family (which has continued for years) and brought to the congregation people who were well informed on issues in the Illinois judicial and prison systems and urged parishioners to write timely letters to those responsible for public policy.

I had personally experienced some of the realities of prison problems when I visited two Grace members who were incarcerated in Illinois state prisons during those years. Both were Grace School graduates whom I had also confirmed. I encouraged our Grace School upper-grades children to write to them in response to their letters, and that helped both members deal with the despair of being forgotten by those on the outside, something they both said was their greatest fear. Andrea Lucht, a physical education teacher whom I admired for her readiness to drum up support for the annual CROP Walk for Hunger was a daughter of the Wayne and Phyllis Lucht family, a social concerns force field all its own. Mark Lucht was the family member who was perpetually advocating causes for any and all on the margins of society. He connected with the Uptown Ministry, the Holy Family congregation in Cabrini Green, and homeless shelters at Grace and other Oak Park congregations — often taking his turn on the 12 a.m. to 7 a.m. shift. Mark served on and chaired the Benevolence Committee at Grace, and his reports at monthly council meetings were challenging, moving, and blessed with the humor of someone who does not take himself too seriously. He had a pickup truck on permanent call to transport mattresses and food to shelter sites, as well as furniture to fire-damaged homes for families all over Chicago. He monitored our mission agency partners at home and abroad with the needed diplomatic touch of keeping recipients responsible with reports back to the congregation accounting for their stewardship. Every congregation needs its share of saints of the Luchts's rank as exemplars of Christ-likeness in ways that are persuasive without being coercive. In my mind, Mark Lucht stood for the many others, known or unknown in congregations, who serve because they're wired to serve by sanctified instinct. He is also a sign of the fullness of the single life — this despite my occasional inquiries about any signs of matrimony on the horizon.

Continuing correspondence with two churchmen from Australia who had been with us at Grace during earlier study sabbaticals led to an invitation to me to visit Concordia Lutheran Seminary and Teachers College in Adelaide. I expanded that invitation into a second sabbatical visit to congregations and schools in Fiji, New Zealand, and Papua New Guinea during February and March 1992. Brief visits to Catholic and Methodist schools on Fiji introduced me to Melanesian church history, which dates from the mid-1800s. Beverly and I also witnessed the obligatory tourist show of Fijians working themselves into a frenzy of animist religious ceremony culminating in a trance-like walk over white-hot stones without wincing. My contacts in New Zealand had come through my Academy of Parish Clergy friend James Glass; they were all Presbyterian clergy in the cities of Christchurch, Arrowtown, Queenstown, and Dunedin.

The incomparable beauty and variety of the South Island matched, if not exceeded, anything Beverly and I had seen anywhere, and the appeal of a slower pace of life showed in the hospitality we found in the parsonage of Rev. Heather Webster, who welcomed me to her pulpit and whose Scottish accent made her sense of humor all the more appealing. She gave us a crash course in the history of her town of Arrowsmith and made it a point to include a tour of what remained of Chinatown, a string of run-down huts that once housed Chinese workers enslaved there a century before. A day on a sheep farm gave me a glimpse of a way of life I had not seen before, at a point farther south on earth than I had ever been before. The pastor at First Presbyterian in Dunedin, Ian Cairns, was an Old Testament scholar with whom I talked about the combination of pastoral and academic vocations, which made for a stimulating conversation. Cairns suggested that I follow his custom of preaching from a simple lectern instead of the ornate marble pulpit that nearly swamped the chancel, a leftover from previous generations of Scotsmen whose homeland church architecture accentuated the predominance of preaching. The week in Adelaide was a mixture of lectures to students, writing a book on marriage preparation, and exploring the environs where German Lutheran settlers had pioneered a century and a half earlier and planted vineyards now producing some of the finest wines anywhere.

Papua New Guinea was a trip into an entirely different world, where church growth was evident in the packed Good Shepherd Lutheran Church in Port Moresby. Papua New Guinea has 2.8 million Christians — Protestant and Catholic — who represent 97 percent of the nation's 2.9 million population. Lutherans had come as early as the 1880s to establish congregations and schools, which I visited in Lae and Logaweng. Grace Church had provided Kingdom Frontiers assistance to the seminary in Lae, whose president is Dr. Wesley Kigasung, a handsome, soft-spoken man whom I had known during his graduate student days at the Lutheran School of Theology in Chicago. He introduced me to students after evening worship in the chapel, a building distinctive for its neatly thatched roof and magnificent altar carved from native hardwood. The students with whom I spoke that evening remembered Ralph Gehrke, whose Bible studies in the Pentateuch and prophets were as valuable to seminarians in Lae as they were to us at Grace Church fifteen years earlier. I spent a day with a pastor well out into the thick forests from Lae, comparing notes on ministry in our respective parts of the world. He made the rounds to his members on foot or bicycle when there were roads, and he described instances of exorcism as a staple of his ministry in a culture where the presence of the demonic is palpable. At Logaweng, the most beautiful seminary site I have ever seen, set a thousand feet up from the Coral Sea, the days spent with missionary hosts Paul and Phyllis Bredin renewed my awareness, among other things, of the value of theological libraries and books. Both were in short supply in this seminary that prepares pastors for some of the most remote areas of Papua New Guinea.

The seminary also provided a view of the beach where my Marine Corps brother-in-law had come ashore to fight the Japanese during World War II. I went swimming in those waters and nearly put an early end to my sabbatical and my life then and there when a wind shift turned the current against me and made me struggle with all I had to make it safely back to shore. At Goroku to the north and west, I spent the better part of a day at the Melanesian Institute, a research program led by a Dutch pastor and an Italian priest, both veterans of years of study and research on the interaction of faith and culture there. Listening to them filled my head with too much to digest in a day and my suitcase with too much to carry as reading material for the long flight to Los Angeles and then back home to Chicago.

We were back home at Grace for Holy Week 1993 and the first weeks of the Easter season before we left for the second part of the sabbatical to retreat locations in France and Scotland. I had visited Taizé twice earlier, but neither occasion was long enough to absorb the uniqueness of "that place of springtime for the spirit," as Pope John XXIII had named it. This time we had a full week to take in the daily rhythms of the Word, prayer, silence, and talk with young adults from throughout Europe, led by the resident brothers of the community. It was April in southeastern France, and the tiny village of Taizé was swamped with thousands of pilgrims who come from near and far to the tents, spare dormitory, and cavernous, simply adorned sanctuary that accommodates the thousands who are drawn to the silence and the powerful chants that are the Taizé trademark worldwide. My sister and brother-in-law were with Beverly and me, and our presence hiked the actuarial average considerably among this mostly under-thirty crowd. The highlight was a brief conversation with Brother Roger Schutz, the founder of Taizé in the post–World War II years, looking obviously older — but still trim — than the man I remembered from a 1950 meeting at a Christian student work camp in Mainz-Kastel, Germany. I asked him to conclude our visit with prayer. In keeping with the Taizé tradition of brevity and simplicity, he prayed, "Lord, prepare us for resurrection." I have remembered those five words many times since and repeated the prayer often with its endless expanse of meaning and application.

The week at Iona, off the southwest coast of Scotland, provided a different, and more ancient, setting. In A.D. 562, St. Columba was driven from his native Ireland to sail alone in his tiny boat until he could no longer see the homeland he loved. The community of prayer and mission he began on Iona has gone through many changes over the centuries, but the incentive it once provided for the mission to the European mainland, while enduring bloody attacks by the Vikings, now took the form of retreat weeks for pilgrims surviving the acids of modernity.

What I gained at Iona was the inspiration of the setting and the prayers. With its treeless hills and rocky beaches, Iona sits like an anchor amid the clouds, wind, and sea that churn around it, historical in every corner of its length, which pilgrims walk each Wednesday, stopping at way stations for prayer and quiet. It was not the songs, as at Taizé, but the language of the prayers that reached me deeply. The daily Matins and Vespers intercessions were written by people from the Church of Scotland during more recent years, since the renovation of Iona by Ian McCloud and others in the 1940s. I had read about Iona since my seminary days and had continued my interest in it as a place of Christian renewal in Europe after World War II, along with Sigtuna in Sweden, Bochum in Germany, and Bossey in Switzerland, and Taizé. I had wanted to visit Iona in particular because of its fourteen-century tradition as an oasis for the soul. Places of retreat were on my mind and set me up for a dream I experienced on our last night at Iona.

I am little experienced in dreams as a means of God's speaking, and I lack any well-developed theology of dreams. But what came to me in my sleep that last night at Iona was so vivid that I awakened Beverly to tell her of my dream: a retreat house awaiting us when we returned to the United States. At that hour she wasn't much interested; but the next morning she heard me out as we returned to London for our flight home. It was a house on Washington Island, Wisconsin, that came onto the screen of my subconscious that last night at Iona, one that I had seen when visiting the island one day in the early 1970s. I had a clear memory of the magnificent beams that supported the great room around which the rest of the mansion was built, and now I envisioned it as a retreat house for Grace Lutheran Church. When we got back, I shared my Iona dream with the elders, who wisely suggested that I test whether my idea of funding it entirely from donors outside Grace Church was a pipe dream or the real thing. I had learned that it was for sale by its owner, a partner in the same firm in which our son, Christopher, was an attorney. I set out on a two-year quest for funding — and came up empty. But Chris knew of my interest, and when the time was right for him, he approached his colleague with a proposal to buy it himself. He did so and has been generous in making it available for annual summer retreats led by Martin Marty and me since 1995. What began with a dream on a sabbatical visit to Iona has become a place of dreams for many, a splendid retreat setting for renewal of soul and body for those who have found it an extension of Iona on another island, this one a few miles out into Lake Michigan.

Marty, closest of close friends since our seminary days in 1947, shared another dream a year later. On Easter Sunday 1993, we took a walk after our families finished dinner at the parsonage table. I spoke not of a dream but of an idea about retirement, since my upcoming sixty-fifth birthday made me think about it more concretely. Neither of us had imminent plans, but both of us knew it was a good idea to plan well ahead. I mentioned 1998, five years ahead when I would turn 70, as a time I had in mind. He said little about the date but put into five words a piece of advice I took and have passed on to many since: "Define yourself by your future." I let that phrase settle in with its healthy implications that my future was in God's hands, that my ministry at Grace would end, but not my future in ministry, that I need not replicate the horror stories of retired pastors hanging on too long in "their" parishes as pests, and that some new scenario linking past and future ministry could occur in God's good time and way. That Easter afternoon conversation had a future.

In the mid-1990s, three important developments took place at Grace Church. The first was a "Goals for Grace Church" retreat in April 1995, which brought together the parish leadership for a two-day exploration of goals in four areas: church family (inreach), neighbors (outreach), growth, and worship. These are terms that can be cliches of a church meeting when they are stranded in the obvious or the irrelevant, or they can be minefields of combat when tunnel-vision Christians collide on what kind of growth and what kind of worship. Retreat leader Brian Becker, fresh from Tent Sale leadership and already well on his way in leadership training as a profession, was aware of both pitfalls. He helped us avoid both fog and impasse with a process of strategies to connect with where we were and whither we were tending as a congregation in 1995.

By this time I had worked with the elders on a timetable for my stepping down (the word "retirement" didn't work) and helping the parish plan for new pastoral leadership. To that end, we engaged Peter Steinke, a Lutheran pastor with parish experience who had moved into a specialized ministry as a congregation-watcher and consultant with enough savvy to keep clergy and parishes from living in denial of the hard issues and enough care to help both move ahead constructively. His month with us was productive: he looked us over from top to bottom, perceived our flaws, and supported our strengths. The general areas of the "Goals" conference became the framework for more specific planning, especially in the matter of preparing to call my successor.

The second important move was a follow-up on the study of space needs that was done in the late 1980s. We had not hurried the process toward decision on renovating the current plant or adding a new wing. It was better to find that answer by allowing time for all of us to see which was the better choice. At first the perception was that Grace School was the primary reason for adding a new wing, but it became clear that the school was only part of the reason. No less real were the needs for additional offices, meeting rooms, storage, and "people space," where believers could assemble, converse, and sometimes console and counsel each other. Things progressed as a series of assignments were made in specific areas: for the building needs, the finances, communication and publicity, and the possible need to purchase new land. Brian Becker worked with congregation president Dan Lehmann in overall coordination, and Leon Rosenthal and I provided pastoral support. What meant the most to me throughout those years of planning and meetings was a deepening sense of ownership in ministry by the people of God at Grace Church. While I had made my 1998 date of retirement public in late 1995, I did not have a lame-duck feeling from this surge of lay leadership in major decisions. It confirmed my belief about pastoral ministry from my ordination day onward: God calls pastors to equip his people for ministry. To me it means that a strong pastorate is necessary for a strong laity, as pastor and people together draw strength from Christ, the Head of the whole body.

Well along in the procession of all-member meetings to decide on major items, another serendipitous gift of the Holy Spirit gave our spirits a huge boost. It was in 1997, and the subject was whether we could afford the sizable cost of adding the air-conditioning present in the sanctuary to the plans for the new wing. The debate that followed was earnest and respectful of both sides of the question: too self-serving of our own comforts or too short-sighted about prospects not likely to enter the oven of summer Sunday heat. When my turn to speak came, I rose to say that I had been looking for an angel who might cover this item without subtracting it from a previous commitment. I added that to date no such angel had been found, and that perhaps the best thing to do would be to wait until one appeared. I paused briefly after making that suggestion, having nothing better to offer, and a small voice from the back of the room — so soft that I didn't even hear it — announced: "You've found your angel." I had to ask someone what had caused the sudden eruption of applause, cheers, tears, and a standing ovation. I wasn't entirely surprised that Eleanor Schmider was the only person sitting, blushing but also beaming, in the back row. Moments like that infused an electrifying spark into a daunting campaign, and it boosted our spirits with the demonstration of the faith active in love that would prove to be more than sufficient to see us through.

The third event of major importance in the mid-1990s was Phyllis Kersten. She accepted the congregation's call to become our associate pastor in 1996, after Leon Rosenthal left to become pastor of Wilmette Lutheran Church on Chicago's north shore. I had known and admired Phyllis during her earlier ten years of service with the Lutheran Church–Missouri Synod mission department during its halcyon years from 1963 to 1974, followed by her eight years on the Wheat Ridge Ministries staff. When she brought the wealth of her gifts and experience to her mid-life readiness for ordination after completing seminary training, I was eager for her to join us at Grace. She was installed on July 14, 1996, and became the first ordained woman to serve on the pastoral staff at Grace. Together we presented a new sight in the Grace chancel, not just because of the contrast of male and female pastors but because I was a foot taller than Phyllis. Prior to her call, I had asked for several informational meetings of the congregation to deal with biblical and confessional questions about the ordination of women. But more than that, I wanted to emphasize that it was not Phyllis's gender but her qualities of mind and spirit that were reasons to call her as our associate pastor. In the call meeting that followed there were no objections; the vote was unanimous. The only negative sentiment had come well before that meeting, from one of our older homebound members: she told me there was no way she would receive Holy Communion "from that lady pastor." I took Pastor Kersten along with me to introduce her to our shut-ins after her installation, including the one where a welcome was not assured. Phyllis followed up with pastoral visits of her own a few weeks later. The next time I came to call on the objecting parishioner myself, her opening comment was, "Why did you wait so long to call Pastor Kersten, anyway?" I knew that the last possible objection to "the lady pastor" was behind us. Phyllis Kersten was among the main reasons that my concluding two years at Grace were sheer bonus all the way.

While the pace quickened toward 1998, there were still those moments of surprise in ministry that kept me buoyed in the daily work. At a black-tie dinner I was attending downtown, the evening began with the alarming collapse of the woman who was chairing the event. All of us were relieved when she was revived and taken to the hospital, but that reminder of our mortality still hung in the air. The seating arrangements had put me next to Jim Lehrer, an honoree that evening. He initiated conversation with a question about my line of work, and when I told him what it was, he looked surprised and quipped that it was a first for him to see a tuxedo-clad Lutheran preacher. His tone turned serious, however, when he leaned forward and said, "I want to know what you believe about death." He spoke of the death of his father when he was a teenager and the unresolved loss it had been for him since. With candor that I did not expect, he went on to describe the dilemma his wife and daughters had with death as a taboo subject around their dinner table, even after he had nearly died of a heart attack some years earlier. Intending to reflect faith, hope, and brevity in my response to this man who speaks to millions nightly on the Jim Lehrer News Hour, I said, "Death is a conquered enemy." Our conversation on what that meant continued in earnest throughout the dinner hour.

After the awards ceremony, Lehrer excused himself to go back to his hotel room to continue work on a novel he was writing. But before he left, he asked for my card. A year or more later, I received a gift copy of the novel he had been working on that evening, with his note of appreciation for what he termed a life-changing turn in his outlook on death and life. The experience taught me once again the importance of being ready when asked for a reason for the hope within us.

November 19, 1995, was a happy day at Grace: the campaign for the new wing, labeled Vision for Grace, was launched at a parish-wide dinner that was held, appropriately enough, in Concordia College's Geiseman Memorial Gymnasium. Our relationship with Concordia had improved greatly with the arrival of George Heider as the new president; he had become a friend and partner to me in every possible way we could find for cooperation. That day we heard the stirring challenge of the goal of paying for the new wing; but the greater emphasis was on the expansion of vision for divine grace in the expanded ministry to which God was calling us, as some four hundred people of the parish became involved at every level of the campaign. Building estimates did go up, of course, but with the stellar leadership of Ken Folgers as chair of the Building Committee, the upward curve did not go off the chart. And equally strong leadership from Brian Becker, Judy Reinhardt, and Christa Krout kept the army of Grace committee workers on track; pledges neared four million as the groundbreaking approached. The few shovelfuls of dirt from the south lawn of the church on March 29, 1998, the Fifth Sunday in Lent, soon gave way to the huge excavation for the foundation of the new wing, and the year-long building of the new structure was underway.

In January 1998, the search for a new pastor began, with Stephen Schmidt chairing the Call Committee of nine, who at the outset had little idea of the marathon of seventy-four meetings that lay ahead in their process of winnowing the candidate field from one hundred down to the dozen who were invited for personal interviews. They did their work with exceeding thoroughness, and they had the benefit of ex-officio input from Pastors Phyllis Kersten and Victor Brandt, a part-time pastoral staff member who for the previous year and a half had blessed the congregation with the leaven of his years in the ministry. It was not appropriate for me to participate in the Call Committee meetings; but it was appropriate for me to spend time with each of the candidates before each one met with the committee and to offer my personal glimpse of the immense privilege of serving the people of Grace.

During these late winter and early spring months of 1998, plans were in full stride because Pentecost Sunday, May 31, 1998, was to be my last Sunday as pastor of the congregation. Julie Christopher, a Grace member in her twenties — another sign of promising younger parish leadership — took on the logistics of planning the place and program for the retirement dinner, to be held Friday evening, May 29. It came much faster than I could get my head and heart to prepare for it. And when it did arrive, it was an outpouring of faith, hope, and, above all, love — love shown to Dean and Beverly Lueking. Speakers spoke, and a video presented cameo messages from our family. The Lueking Continuing Ministry Fund was announced. I spoke of my gratitude in words altogether inadequate to what I felt in my heart. The band played, and we danced until late in the evening. And the 666 Grace members and friends who came that evening went home with peace in their hearts, and no sign of the beast on any forehead — or anywhere.

A parable of the blessing poured out on me and the congregation that final Pentecost Sunday came in a surprising moment during the distribution of Holy Communion: I spoke a blessing on Audrey Wayne, a beautiful, auburn-haired child of eight who stood beside her mother in the procession of communicants. And as I did, she looked up at me and, with no small gesture of courage, put her arms around my waist and gave me a hug. Audrey was giving a blessing back to me, all spontaneous with the pure beauty that children convey best. It brought tears to my eyes — this sign of the goodness of God's love given to me by the congregation for the forty-four years since that August Sunday of my ordination, when others had laid their hands of blessing on my head. The pericope lesson from Acts 2 was exactly right for sermon theme, "Come, Creator Spirit," with the promise of the Paraclete to guide Grace Church into an abundant future, even as it had in the past. I managed to get through most of the sermon without an emotional overflow, until the last sentence, which, though spoken with an uneven voice, delivered what I wanted to offer:

> In gratitude and affection, beloved people of Grace, my joy and crown, my spiritual family and ever my heart's home, I commend you to the Lord Jesus in the power of the Holy Spirit to build you up and keep your heats and minds united with mine in the peace of God which passes all understanding.

The Grace Senior Choir sang a Bach cantata, *Komm Heiliger Geist,* in the afternoon Vespers, and after the homily was preached, we sang "O Day Full of Grace." I chanted the closing benediction. Pentecost Sunday, a day that had been indeed filled with grace, had come to a close. And as it did, my service as pastor of Grace Lutheran Church ended, after forty-four years filled with divine grace beyond all I could ask or think.

A season of grace had ended, but as it always is with seasons of grace, in its ending was another beginning.

Epilogue

Being named pastor emeritus by the people of Grace Church gave me a bridge to a continuing ministry in new ways and places. Since the fall of 1998, during the autumn and spring semesters, I have been teaching seminarians of the Evangelical Church of the Augsburg Confession, as Lutherans are called in Bratislava, Slovakia. I teach in English — with the help of interpreters and the patience of the 220 students who bear with me — because I do not speak Slovak. Beverly speaks it fluently. Thus many heads nod affirmatively that it's about time I keep quiet and let her do the talking as we get around in this beautiful little country wedged in between East and West in central Europe. We are taking this new chapter in our lives one year at a time. I genuinely enjoy this new opportunity to pass on to seminarians the best of my Grace years while teaching and learning with them.

We do not enjoy the absence from children and grandchildren for half the year; but the unusual fact that all our children — Ann and husband Douglas Anderson and their four sons, Sarah and husband Mark McCabe and their daughter, and our sons Christopher and Joel — live within a half hour of us when we are home gives us no reason to complain. Being near them during the winter and summer months after being overseas for the fall and spring semesters helps us count the blessings of their proximity. And being several thousand miles away from

Grace Church for half of every year since I retired in 1998 has been a
positive reason why the transition from the long Grace pastorate to new
ministry opportunities has gone well. It has allowed the new pastor at
Grace Church, Bruce Modahl, a clearer path toward establishing himself in his pastoral role. The good rapport between the two of us when I
am home is a result of the simple but essential basics that we both agree
on (and the congregation understands): I do no pastoral ministry at
Grace unless he assigns or approves it; neither of us tolerates gossip or
any hint of undermining each other; and we both enjoy finding new
ways to work together for the good of the parish.

Another form of ministry that has opened up to me over the past
three years is serving as a pastoral advisor to staff people of Opportunity International in Russia and the Balkans, plus teaching courses in
servant leadership to World Vision staff people in eastern Europe and
South Africa. Both organizations provide modest loans to help impov-
erished people develop small businesses (the payback rate is 97 percent
worldwide) and flourish spiritually through renewal in the Christian
faith. I continue to do occasional teaching, preaching, and summer retreats. I do these things because I love doing them, and I don't mind being sometimes regarded as someone who has flunked retirement.

What have I learned from the immense privilege of serving the people of Grace? What do I hope will continue strong long after I am gone?
The following come to mind:

- The heart and soul of ministry is Jesus Christ, crucified and risen,
  who is the Good News for every bad situation, whether in the ups
  and downs of the congregation or in the life of the world he calls us
  to serve, personally and together with the whole church for the
  whole family of humankind.
- Love for people, Christ-given love applied to people, no matter
  what, is the sure sign of the awesome calling to stand before God in
  their behalf and to stand before people in his behalf.
- Pastoral ministry is by its very nature collegial. Despite our sins of
  the unholy trinity of me, myself, and I, pastoral ministry is partnership with others, called to serve in the freedom of the Holy Spirit's

marvelous ways of using each for the good of the other, and all together for the common good of the congregation.

- Each congregation, like each human being, has a unique face, which needs to be discerned with wisdom and encouraged with patience. Our unique gifts at Grace include gifted laity, Grace School, and the ministry of music. Every congregation on earth, whether small or massive in size and scope, has unique gifts, and happy are the pastor and parish who work together to discover, nurture, and celebrate them.

- The congregation itself is the primary place for pastoral growth in the art and skills of ministry of the Word, through the ordinariness and the extraordinariness of the daily rounds, through conflict and reconciliation, through failure and success, through hard work and the wonderful surprises that come with letting go and letting others lead.

- There are no ordinary people, believer or unbeliever, interesting or dull, well known or forgettable, young or old. Every person has a story to be woven into the seamless garment in which the Lord clothes his Body, the church.

- The joy that sometimes crowns our daily work today is a sign of that coming fullness of joy when faith becomes sight, hope is realized in full, and love shall be made perfect in the presence of our Lord Jesus, the great Shepherd of the sheep.